HOW TO USE RESEARCH EVIDENCE WELL IN EDUCATION

This book provides education professionals with an accessible and actionable guide to using research well in real-world contexts.

Using research evidence to improve education is critically important but often poorly supported. There is little or no guidance for educators and leaders about how to do it well. Through practical examples, school case studies, improvement activities and practice checklists, this book unpacks what using research well involves and shows you how to develop it as an action-based practice within your work. The book's easy-to-read chapters guide you through the process of: identifying your purpose for using research and finding appropriate research, engaging with the research thoughtfully and implementing it effectively, and modelling and supporting quality research use within your organisation.

Written for teachers and leaders across all stages of education who want to use research evidence better within their work, this is an indispensable addition to the professional library.

Mark Rickinson, Professor, Faculty of Education, Monash University, Australia.

Lucas Walsh, Professor, Faculty of Education, Monash University, Australia.

Joanne Gleeson, Researcher, Faculty of Education, Monash University, Australia.

Blake Cutler, Researcher and PhD Candidate, Faculty of Education, Monash University, Australia.

Bernice Plant, Research Fellow, BehaviourWorks Australia, Monash University, Australia.

Mark Boulet, Senior Research Fellow, BehaviourWorks Australia, Monash University, Australia.

Genevieve Hall, PhD Graduate, Faculty of Education, Monash University, Australia.

Connie Cirkony, Senior Lecturer, Faculty of Education, Monash University, Australia.

Mandy Salisbury, Researcher and PhD Candidate, Faculty of Education, Monash University, Australia.

"I have had continuous educational research funding from a few thousand to many millions of dollars for almost 40 years, and I learned a huge amount from this excellent collaboration between educators in schools and members of the university academy. Unlike many other books on evidence use in education, this highly readable and usable book is not doctrinaire about promoting some kinds of research over others, it is not driven by political agendas or commercial interests, and its authors do not blow their own trumpets. It's a beautifully humble book with depth, integrity, credibility, and practicality. Read it. Use it. You'll love it as much as I did."

Andy Hargreaves, Research Professor, Boston College

"The days of evidence are over. The days of interpreting and making wise use of evidence are upon us. This is the must-read book for educators striving to make informed, impactful evidence-based decisions. Following the great success of the Q Project, this book is rich in practical strategies, real-school examples, and actionable insights. It heralds a new, fresh, and powerful way of using and interpreting the myriads of evidence claims that permeate our schools."

John Hattie, Laureate Professor Emeritus, University of Melbourne

"Using research evidence to inform teaching is a goal of education systems across the world - but there is often little or no guidance about how to do it well. This book changes that. It is an accessible, hands-on guide based on years of work in the field that brings together an actionable framework for educators and decision-makers with concrete examples and tools. The goal: nothing less than helping improve teaching quality and, ultimately, student outcomes."

Tracey Burns, Chief of Global Strategy and Research,
US National Center on Education and the Economy

"At its best, research can empower educators, allowing them to combine their own professional expertise with the insights, experiences and outcomes of many others across education systems. This book tackles the hardest challenge in educational research – how to move from accessing research to using it effectively. The practical examples and thoughtful discussion make this an indispensable resource in ensuring that research actually changes lives."

Jon Kay, Head of Evidence Synthesis, UK Education Endowment Foundation

"Too often evidence-informed practice is presented as a top-down process in which teachers merely implement research findings without recognising the importance of critical engagement and context-specific application. This book is vastly different in that it puts educational professionals at the heart of evidence-informed practice, truly empowers them to engage critically with research evidence and challenges them to apply it appropriately to their contexts. An essential guide for anyone who wants to start using evidence *well* in their settings."

Lisa-Maria Müller, Head of Research and Policy,
UK Chartered College of Teaching

"This book is an essential resource for educators and leaders committed to using research effectively to enhance their professionalism and their practice. Each chapter expertly guides readers through critical elements of how to use research well, from implementation to continuous improvement, and equips them with practical tools to sustain and model this essential work. It will be an invaluable asset for all educators seeking to leverage research and their own expertise to drive meaningful and sustainable improvements in practice."

Barbara Waterston, CEO, Australian Council for Educational Leaders

"As school leaders, it is imperative that we quarantine time to consider research evidence before developing new initiatives that we think might improve student outcomes. Spending time as a leadership team to better understand the barriers, and use research well to inform school improvement work is critical to achieving sustained outcomes. This book helps to ensure that the time school leaders spend engaging with evidence is time well spent. Its practical guidance and rich examples support school improvement teams to get on the same page about the relevance of evidence to their work, and develop smart and efficient ways of working with it."

Carrie Wallis, Principal, Wantirna College, Melbourne

"Using research evidence effectively to improve outcomes in schools is an essential undertaking for school leaders committed to evidence-informed improvement. Mark Rickinson and his colleagues not only highlight the importance of research but also showcase powerful examples of successful implementation from practitioners. The focus on the 'how' makes this book invaluable, bridging the gap between theory and real-world impact. A must read for educators looking to turn research into meaningful change in schools!"

Pitsa Binnion, PSM, Former Principal, McKinnon Secondary College, Melbourne

HOW TO USE RESEARCH EVIDENCE WELL IN EDUCATION

A GUIDE FOR EDUCATORS AND LEADERS

Mark Rickinson, Lucas Walsh,
Joanne Gleeson, Blake Cutler,
Bernice Plant, Mark Boulet,
Genevieve Hall, Connie Cirkony
and Mandy Salisbury

Designed cover image: Rodney Dekker/Aspire Pictures

First published 2026
by Routledge
4 Park Square, Milton Park, Abingdon, Oxon OX14 4RN

and by Routledge
605 Third Avenue, New York, NY 10158

Routledge is an imprint of the Taylor & Francis Group, an informa business

© 2026 Mark Rickinson, Lucas Walsh, Joanne Gleeson, Blake Cutler, Bernice Plant, Mark Boulet, Genevieve Hall, Connie Cirkony, Mandy Salisbury

The right of Mark Rickinson, Lucas Walsh, Joanne Gleeson, Blake Cutler, Bernice Plant, Mark Boulet, Genevieve Hall, Connie Cirkony, Mandy Salisbury to be identified as authors of this work has been asserted in accordance with sections 77 and 78 of the Copyright, Designs and Patents Act 1988.

The Open Access version of this book, available at www.taylorfrancis.com, has been made available under a Creative Commons Attribution-Non Commercial-No Derivatives (CC-BY-NC-ND) 4.0 license.

Any third party material in this book is not included in the OA Creative Commons license, unless indicated otherwise in a credit line to the material. Please direct any permissions enquiries to the original rightsholder.

Funded by the Paul Ramsay Foundation as part of the Monash Q Project.

Trademark notice: Product or corporate names may be trademarks or registered trademarks, and are used only for identification and explanation without intent to infringe.

British Library Cataloguing-in-Publication Data
A catalogue record for this book is available from the British Library

ISBN: 9781032451947 (hbk)
ISBN: 9781032451930 (pbk)
ISBN: 9781003375845 (ebk)

DOI: 10.4324/9781003375845

Typeset in Helvetica
by KnowledgeWorks Global Ltd.

This book is dedicated to the teachers and school leaders who made this work possible and whose insights are its backbone.

CONTENTS

List of Illustrations xi
Acknowledgements xiii

1 Introduction – Using Research Well   1
2 Identifying a Clear Purpose   17
3 Selecting Appropriate Research   41
4 Engaging with Research Thoughtfully   67
5 Implementing Research Thoughtfully   95
6 Modelling Quality Research Use   117
7 Supporting Quality Research Use   139
8 Conclusion – Continuing the Journey   161

Appendices 169
Index 197

LIST OF ILLUSTRATIONS

FIGURES

1.1	Quality Use of Research Evidence (QURE) Framework (Source: Rickinson et al., 2020, p.6)	4
2.1	ATACT Framework (adapted from Presseau et al., 2019)	35
2.2	ATACT Framework with promotion opportunity prompts	37
5.1	Research use collaboration continuum	105

TABLES

1.1	How this book responds to the characteristics of using research well	8
1.2	Structure of the book	9
1.3	How to get the most out of this book	11
2.1	Benefits of consulting others to gather and analyse evidence	21
2.2	Examples of factors to consider and respond to when selecting a specific need	22
2.3	Examples of questions that will provide information to help explain the purpose of research use	24
3.1	Ways that research can support your practice	44
3.2	Contextual factors that may be important for appraising research	45
3.3	Common markers of trustworthiness used by educators	47
3.4	Formats of research and why educators believe they may be useful	49
3.5	Different sources of research	51
3.6	Operators and how they can be used in search strings	53
4.1	Helpful questions to ask of research	70
4.2	Possible factors to consider in your adaptation of research	76
4.3	Examples of components of a research-informed change initiative	79
5.1	Three aspects of implementation readiness	98
5.2	Implementation plan outline	100
5.3	Benefits of trialling a research-informed initiative	103
5.4	Considerations for engaging others during implementation	105
6.1	Examples of external sources of support for research use	122
7.1	Examples of meetings where research use can be discussed and implemented	142
7.2	Examples of research-related resources	143

CASE STUDIES

2.1	What does identifying a clear purpose look like in action?	27
3.1	What does selecting appropriate research look like in action?	56
4.1	What does engaging thoughtfully with research look like in action?	81
5.1	What does thoughtful implementation look like in action?	107
6.1	What does modelling quality research use look like in action?	128
7.1	What does supporting quality research use look like in action?	150

APPENDICES

Appendix 1 Introduction - Using Research Well	169
Appendix 2 Identifying a Clear Purpose	171
Appendix 3 Selecting Appropriate Research	175
Appendix 4 Engaging with Research Thoughtfully	181
Appendix 5 Implementing Research Thoughtfully	185
Appendix 6 Modelling Quality Research Use	189
Appendix 7 Supporting Quality Research Use	193

ACKNOWLEDGEMENTS

The authors would like to acknowledge:

- the Wurundjeri and Bunurong Peoples of the Kulin Nation as the traditional owners and custodians of the lands on which this work was undertaken;
- the many Australian teachers, school leaders and system leaders who took part in this work and brought it to life despite the many other demands on their time;
- colleagues at the Paul Ramsay Foundation (John Bush, Maria Simonelli, Clare Hodgson, Laura Bird, Galina Laurie and the wider team) for believing in and supporting this project;
- Q Project team members (Phoebe Marshall, Komal Daredia, Adriana Capponi, Hang Khong and Darlene McGown) for their collegiality and communications and project management expertise;
- Q Project School Advisory Group members (Amelia Apogremiotis, Brisbane Boys' College; Cathy Crouch, Aurora College; Ted Noon, Ashcroft High School; Eleanor Wilkinson, Heatley State School; Megan Ganter, Manchester Primary School; Maria Alberto, Xavier College and Steven Kolber, Brunswick Secondary College) for their advice and suggestions during the early development of this book;
- Q Project research partners, Steering Committee members, Jurisdiction Group members, Stakeholder Reference Group members and national and international collaborators for their varied expertise and sustained support during the lifetime of the project;
- Professor Liam Smith, Director of BehaviourWorks Australia, for his early contributions to the Q Project and ongoing support;
- the design team at Blueboat (Emma Baird, Ros Strong and Nicole McKenzie) and the copy editor (Peter Symons) for their expert inputs to this book; and
- the Faculty of Education and Monash University for their encouragement and support for this project.

CHAPTER 1
INTRODUCTION – USING RESEARCH WELL

USING RESEARCH WELL INVOLVES YOU:
- shifting your focus from whether you use research to how well you use research.

USING RESEARCH WELL IS IMPORTANT BECAUSE:
- it is professionally rewarding for educators; and
- it enables educational improvement for students.

USING RESEARCH WELL HELPS TO AVOID:
- research-informed improvement initiatives that are ineffective; and
- an organisational culture that is either reactive or static.

THIS CHAPTER WILL HELP YOU TO:
- appreciate what using research well means and why it matters; and
- understand how this book can help you and your colleagues.

LEARN MORE ABOUT USING RESEARCH WELL BY:
- reading the chapter's main sections;
- completing the improvement activity; and
- exploring Appendix 1 for further activities and reading.

INTRODUCTION

"Why are our students getting these outcomes? We are working so hard, what can we do differently?"

These were the simple but challenging questions facing Phoebe and Alex,[1] a Principal and leading teacher within a small Australian primary school in a community experiencing disadvantage.

They both knew that "if we want to change the trajectory of our students and our current practices are not working" then "we need to think outside the box ... to find different ways that would set our teachers and students up for success".

But to do this, they also recognised that "we needed to make sure that we weren't just following the latest fad" and instead "actually did our homework to understand how well-researched certain practices were".

It was this strong sense of wanting to avoid fads and understand the research base of possible practices, then, that set Phoebe and Alex "down the path of looking at research evidence".

Over the last six years, we have met hundreds of educators like Phoebe and Alex who have genuinely challenging educational needs to respond to and see research evidence as a resource that could help them.

For all too many, though, the process of trying to identify relevant and useful research and then work with colleagues to understand and implement it is not only challenging but also poorly supported. This book is a direct response to this reality that using research evidence in practice is complex, and *there is often little or no guidance for educators and leaders about how to do it well.*

Based on the first study internationally to investigate the idea of quality use of research (or using research well) in schools, it aims to provide busy education professionals with an accessible and actionable guide to the process of using research well in real-world contexts. Put simply, our goal is to show you how using research in practice can be both educationally impactful and professionally rewarding. We want to enable more educators and leaders to have a research use journey like Phoebe and Alex.

Phoebe and Alex sourced some international research on teaching students from backgrounds of poverty that they felt went "hand-in-hand" with their context and needs.

They were able to use this research to better understand the adverse childhood experiences of their own students and the influences these can have on teacher-student interactions, and to initiate professional conversations with staff about "our perceptions of poverty and our openness to change". These conversations then informed how they trialled specific strategies from the research in their classrooms through professional inquiry cycles.

Through this approach, they saw "early stage" positive impacts on classroom practice, such as a fourfold increase in proactive and positive teacher-student interactions and a 50% decrease in reactive or negative interactions.

Drawing on many different real-life examples like this one, this book unpacks what using research well involves and shows you how to develop it as an action-based practice within your work.

At its heart, this book is an invitation to be open to a subtle, but significant, shift in how we think, talk and act in relation to using research evidence in education. That is, to ask ourselves honestly how willing and able we are to shift our focus from *whether we use research* to the more productive question of *how well we use research*.

This shift is easy to say but hard to do, so let's explore:

- what using research well means;
- why it matters; and
- how it can be complex.

Afterwards, we can then turn to what this book provides in response, what it is based on and how it can help you in your setting.

WHAT USING RESEARCH WELL MEANS

Educational practice can be informed by many different types of evidence, but this book is focused specifically on *research evidence*. This means evidence generated through systematic studies undertaken by universities or research organisations and reported in books, reports, articles, research summaries, training courses or events (Nelson et al., 2017).[2]

Educators can both engage in research (i.e., doing research) and engage with research (i.e., using research), but this book is focused specifically on *using research*. This means the process of actively engaging with and drawing on research evidence to inform, change and improve decision making and practice (Coldwell et al., 2017). This process can be undertaken in different ways, and this book is concerned with what it means to *use research well*.

Drawing on the Quality Use of Research Evidence (QURE) Framework developed by the Monash Q Project, using research well (or quality use of research) can be defined at its core as:

> *thoughtful engagement with and implementation of appropriate research evidence (Rickinson et al., 2020, p. 6),"*

It is important to add, though, that using research well also needs to be "supported by a blend of individual and organisational enabling components within a complex system"

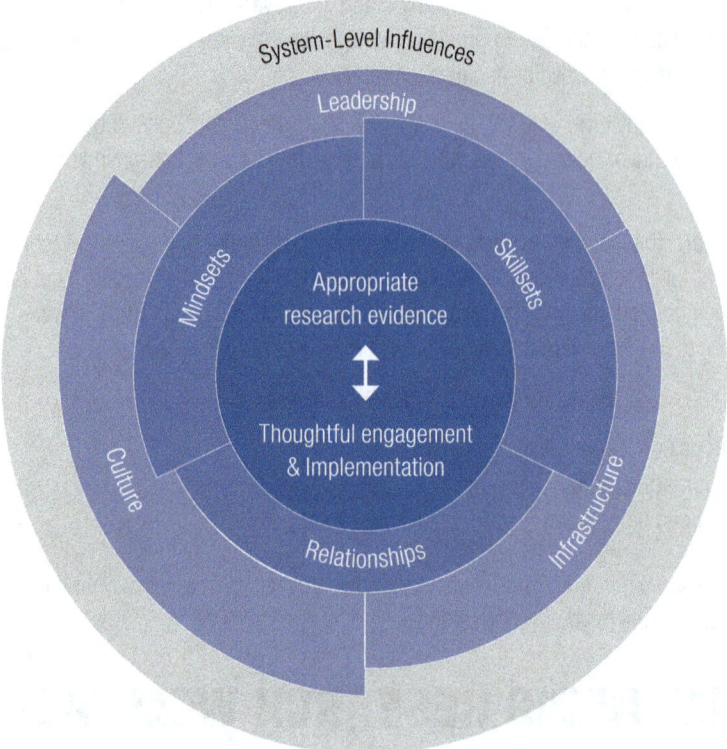

Figure 1.1. *Quality Use of Research Evidence (QURE) Framework (Source: Rickinson et al., 2020, p. 6)*

(Rickinson et al., 2020, p. 6). As shown in Figure 1.1, then, using research well in education comprises:

- two core components (*appropriate research evidence* and *thoughtful engagement and implementation*) which highlight the dual need for the research evidence to be appropriate to context and for our engagement and implementation to be thoughtful;
- three individual enabling components (*skillsets*, *mindsets* and *relationships*) that reflect the skills, dispositions and relations that are required to use research well;
- three organisational enabling components (*culture*, *leadership* and *infrastructure*) that emphasise the need for supportive school leadership, culture and infrastructure; and
- *system-level influences* which underscore how using research well occurs within, and is influenced by, broader systems.

While these components of using research well may sound a little abstract, they are, in fact, strongly connected with educators' experiences of using research in practice.

Let's return to the example of Phoebe and Alex. Their process of introducing research-informed change to improve their students' learning and wellbeing outcomes involved them:

- continually asking questions about "how well does the research fit in our context?" (appropriateness) and looking at "what does the research show us? How can we use it?" (thoughtfulness);
- being motivated by "a curiosity to improve practice to improve student outcomes" (mindsets), collecting and analysing data "to gain as much information about student behaviour as we could" (skillsets) and working with teachers and students to "find a way of cooperating with the highest chance of success" (relationships);
- intentionally "modelling that curiosity and hunger to change the trajectories of students" (leadership), "not adding workload by leveraging data conversations" that were already happening but could be extended to include research (infrastructure) and being clear on "how the research sits beside the organisational and the systemic work that needs to be done" (culture); and
- using their "state department's priorities and standards of evidence" to assess the relevance, feasibility and quality of possible research sources (system-level influences).

Clearly, there is a lot involved in using research well, and so we need to be clear about why it matters.

WHY USING RESEARCH WELL MATTERS

Using research well matters because:

- it builds educators' professionalism;
- it enables educational improvement for students; and
- it strengthens education systems by promoting high-quality use as well as high-quality evidence.

First, using research well matters because it draws on and affirms the professional expertise of educators. As Alex put it, it helps educators "to make conscious decisions about their practice based on research".

Using research well is about recognising the critical importance of integrating professional knowledge from practice with evidence-based insights from research. Using research well, therefore, puts education professionals at the centre, rather than scenarios where "research is used to make decisions by those at the top without giving teachers an opportunity to consider the evidence and to discuss its implications" (Teacher, survey).[3]

A second fundamental reason why using research well is important is its role in enabling educational improvement for students. As one senior leader said very simply:

> *[Quality use of] research matters because kids matter."*

In other words, using appropriate research evidence in thoughtful ways can help teachers and school leaders to make better decisions about which practices will be most beneficial for their students, and how they can best develop and embed those practices in their context. Using research well, then, helps to move schools and systems away from situations where "things would be quickly trialled and abandoned, and practice would stay overall the same" (Teacher, survey).

Finally, using research well matters because it highlights the need for quality use as well as quality research in education systems. Put simply, research-informed improvement requires not only high-quality research but also high-quality use.

The challenge here is that education systems have tended to be far more focused on improving the generation and translation of research evidence (knowledge push) than on strengthening its uptake and use (knowledge pull) (e.g., Gough et al., 2018). As a consequence, there has been insufficient guidance and support for educators about what using research well looks like and how individuals and organisations can get better at it.

Taken together, these three considerations highlight the significance of using research well from the perspective of harnessing the professionalism of educators, driving educational improvement for students and supporting not just quality research but also quality use in systems.

HOW USING RESEARCH WELL CAN BE COMPLEX

As well as understanding why using research well matters, it is also essential to recognise how it can be complex. If this book is an invitation to shift our focus from whether we use research to how well we use research, then what do we need to be aware of to help us make this shift?

There are five characteristics of using research well in education that we need to be aware of: it is sophisticated, integrated and developmental, but it is often hidden and poorly supported.

- *Using research well is a sophisticated practice* – Educators in schools where research is being used well make very clear that the process is a sophisticated and involved one. It is "thoughtful and considered" and involves "a structured approach" that helps "teachers to learn more deeply" and develop and implement "target[ed] initiatives and approaches". Efforts to use research well, therefore, need to embrace and hold on to the professional and nuanced nature of the process.
- *Using research well is an integrated practice* – As one educator put it, using research well "isn't extra work, it's actually asking [colleagues] to think more deeply about the work that they do". This idea is important because it emphasises how the process of using research well is not an add-on but instead is intricately connected with processes

of teaching well and leading well. Efforts to use research well, therefore, need to connect with and build on the wider professional practices of educators and leaders.

- *Using research well is a developmental practice* – Getting better at using research well is an ongoing process both for individuals and for organisations and systems. In the words of one school leader, this is because "acquiring new knowledge and challenging your own knowledge takes time and takes a lot of courage to learn". Efforts to use research well, therefore, need to focus on the importance of ongoing professional learning and long-term capacity building.
- *Using research well is a hidden practice* – The idea of using research well has not been explicitly investigated very much by educational researchers, meaning that its enactment as a practice in schools has often gone unnoticed. As educators explained, there is a need to unpack "the journey of the thinking, the reflecting and the reading" and "be able to describe what it [using research well] looks like". Efforts to use research well, therefore, need to involve it being made more explicit and visible as a practice.
- *Using research well is a poorly supported practice* – Using research well does not happen in a vacuum, but instead needs supportive organisations and systems. To quote a school leader, "there [are] things that departments and systems could do, just like there [are] things that senior leaders in schools need to do to help". All too often, though, the priorities, norms and structures of schools and systems are either ineffective for, or detrimental to, using research well. Efforts to use research well, therefore, need to pay careful attention to the role of organisational enablers and system supports.

RECAP: WHAT USING RESEARCH WELL MEANS, WHY IT MATTERS AND HOW IT CAN BE COMPLEX

The above sections have outlined what using research means, why it matters and how it can be complex.

Using research well:

means "thoughtful engagement with and implementation of appropriate research evidence"

matters because it builds educators' professionalism, enables improvement for students and supports high-quality use in systems

can be complex because it is sophisticated, integrated, developmental, hidden and poorly supported

WHAT THIS BOOK PROVIDES

This book responds directly to each of the five characteristics of using research well that were outlined above.

As shown in Table 1.1, the book contains specific features to help you to develop using research as well as a sophisticated, integrated, developmental process that is explicit and well supported.

Table 1.1.
How this book responds to the characteristics of using research well

Using research well is:	This book responds by:	This is achieved through:
sophisticated	showing how the process is nuanced but also manageable	**Two key practices** within each chapter provide you with an accessible way to engage with the subtleties of using research well.
integrated	showing how the process can connect to current capacity and context	**Diagnostic activities and practice checklists** support you to understand your context and starting points throughout the book.
developmental	showing how the process can be scaffolded and ongoing	**Improvement activities** provide you with prompts, templates, examples and tips to support the continued development of your practice.
hidden	showing what the process involves and looks like in action	**Case studies and behavioural activities** help you to see specific practices in action and to develop them in your own context.
poorly supported	showing how the process can be enabled and supported	**Dedicated chapters** showing how you can model and support different aspects of using research well within your context.

The successive chapters of the book guide you through different aspects of using research well (Table 1.2). Following this opening chapter, there are four chapters that take you through identifying a clear purpose (Chapter 2), selecting appropriate research (Chapter 3), engaging thoughtfully with it (Chapter 4) and implementing it thoughtfully (Chapter 5).

The next two chapters will help you to see how using research well can be modelled (Chapter 6) and supported (Chapter 7). Chapter 8 draws together the key messages of the book and provides pointers for continuing your journey of using research well.

Table 1.2.
Structure of the book

Chapter 1: Introduction - Using Research Well	What is using research well and how can this book help me to do it?
Chapter 2: Identifying a Clear Purpose	What need are we addressing through using research?
Chapter 3: Selecting Appropriate Research	What research are we going to pay attention to?
Chapter 4: Engaging with Research Thoughtfully	How can we engage with research thoughtfully?
Chapter 5: Implementing Research Thoughtfully	How can we implement research thoughtfully?
Chapter 6: Modelling Quality Research Use	How can we demonstrate using research well to others?
Chapter 7: Supporting Quality Research Use	How can we support using research well?
Chapter 8: Conclusion - Continuing the Journey	How can we keep learning about using research well?

All chapters have a common structure that is designed to be easy to read, interesting to engage with and motivating to put into practice. In each chapter, you will find:

- a front-page infographic that summarises the key ideas and contents;
- reflection questions to consider at the start and end of the chapter;
- two key practices which capture how to enact the focus of the chapter;
- recap boxes after each key practice to reinforce key points;
- a school case study to show what the key practices look like in action;
- an improvement activity to help you develop the key practice behaviours in your context; and
- an appendix which provides additional resources, such as a key practices checklist, case studies, key concepts boxes, references and suggested further readings.

For all of these resources, the intention is to provide a menu of options to choose from as opposed to a recipe to follow.

WHAT THIS BOOK IS BASED ON

All of the insights, examples and activities in this book are based on a six-year research study undertaken with schools in Australia between 2019 and 2024 (for more details, see

Rickinson et al., 2024). Supported by the Paul Ramsay Foundation, the Monash Q Project was the first study internationally to investigate the idea of quality use of research (or using research well).

It engaged with over 2,300 teachers, school leaders and system leaders across Australia and internationally, in order to understand: what using research well means, what it looks like in practice, and how it can be developed in schools and systems. This book draws particularly on data generated by three surveys and several rounds of interviews with educators (for more details, see Rickinson et al., 2023, 2024).

You will read, for example, direct quotes from educators' interview comments and open-text responses to our first survey that help to illustrate key ideas about using research well. Common qualitative themes from the interviews and surveys will also be highlighted, along with an indication of their frequency (e.g., referenced in XX% of interviews, XX% of surveys).

You will also hear about certain quantitative findings that point to important patterns in educators' survey responses, such as the percentage endorsing a particular item or the percentage indicating that a particular item was an important component of using research well.

This book also presents behaviour-based insights and approaches that emerged from the Q Project's long-term collaboration with Monash's BehaviourWorks Australia (BWA) research unit. This work explored what using research well looks like as a series of on-the-ground actions and how these can be enabled (for details, see Plant et al., 2022).

Through the improvement activities designed with the BWA team in each chapter, you will learn about identifying and articulating behaviours that are involved in using research well and ways to enact and support positive behaviour change.

HOW THIS BOOK CAN HELP YOU

This book is written for educational professionals who want to use research well to drive improvement that is meaningful and impactful. This includes teachers and leaders of all kinds within schools, but also individuals working with schools, such as system leaders, professional learning providers and evidence brokers.

Importantly, this book is designed to be helpful for people who are new to the idea of using research through to those who are already very experienced with the process. So you might have picked up this book because you:

- are interested in the idea of using research to drive improvement and want practical advice on how to do it well;
- are using a particular research-informed approach but want to know how to make it more impactful in your context;

- want to strengthen the use of research within your team or organisation and are looking for examples of how others have done that; or
- are keen to help educators or schools to evaluate their use of research and need some guidance and ideas of specific practices or capacities to assess.

Whatever your starting point and need, there are four suggestions that will help you to get the most out of this book (Table 1.3).

Table 1.3.
How to get the most out of this book

1. Use it as a workbook	This book is designed to be directly used as a workbook. So to get the most out of it, approach each chapter as an active learning experience and engage with the reflection questions and improvement activities.
2. Use it with others	This book is designed to support connection and collaboration. So to get the most out of it, look for ways to work through it with colleagues and try out its suggested practices within existing teams or groups.
3. Use it in chunks	This book is designed to make the nuanced process of using research well manageable. So to get the most out of it, work on one chapter or part of a chapter at a time and aim for depth of engagement rather than speed of coverage.
4. Use it based on your starting point	This book is designed to enable readers to focus on specific aspects of using research well based on their own needs. So to get the most out of it, use the reflection questions and improvement activities to identify your current practices and areas for improvement.

RECAP: WHAT THIS BOOK PROVIDES, WHAT IT IS BASED ON AND HOW IT CAN HELP YOU

The above sections have explained what this book contains, what it is based on and how it can be used best.

This book:

guides you through different aspects of using research well in easy-to-read chapters with lots of activities and examples

is based on a six-year research study undertaken with schools in Australia between 2019 and 2024

will be most helpful if you use it as a workbook, with others, in chunks and for your particular needs

◉ PUTTING THINGS INTO PRACTICE
WHAT DOES USING RESEARCH WELL MEAN FOR ME, WHERE ARE MY OPPORTUNITIES FOR GROWTH AND HOW CAN I USE THIS BOOK TO IMPROVE?

This final section is designed to help you to move from understanding what using research well means to deciding how you can use this book to develop and improve it within your context.

The following activity takes you through some reflective questions about using research well within your organisational context, and then helps you to think about how you might use the different parts of this book to help you to improve.

You can choose to complete this activity individually and/or with colleagues as a team.

In this section, we also encourage you to:

Look at Appendix 1 where you might like to:

- Engage with Teresa's case study about developing research use through professional learning.
- Read more about the Q Project's work on using research well.

Initiate a group conversation in your school or organisation about using research well. This conversation might involve you comparing and discussing your responses to the improvement activity below.

IMPROVEMENT ACTIVITY
REFLECTING ON USING RESEARCH WELL IN YOUR CONTEXT AND HOW YOU COULD USE DIFFERENT PARTS OF THIS BOOK TO HELP YOU TO IMPROVE

To make the ideas discussed in this chapter more tangible for you, use the space below to respond to some reflective questions about using research well within your context.

What does using research well mean for you in your organisational context?

....
....
....

Why is using research well important to you in your context?

....
....
....

What aspects of using research well in your context do you want to improve?

....
....
....

Use the prompts overleaf to identify aspects of using research well that you want to work on in your context - tick all statements that feel important to you. You will see that there are two blank rows at the bottom for you to record any additional things that you want to improve that are not on the list.

I want to improve how I:	For example, I want to get better at:
☐ identify a purpose for using research	☐ selecting an issue in my context to drive the use of research ☐ communicating my purpose for using research to others
☐ find and select research to use	☐ deciding what research is relevant for my purpose/context ☐ finding research that is trustworthy and useful
☐ engage with research	☐ reading and understanding research more deeply ☐ translating and adapting research for my context
☐ implement research in practice	☐ planning the implementation of a research-informed initiative ☐ trialling new initiatives and involving others in implementation
☐ model using research to others	☐ developing my own research use capacity and practice ☐ demonstrating using research well to others
☐ support others to use research	☐ supporting research use in tangible ways such as through meetings and organisational processes ☐ building a supportive culture such as through collaboration and experimentation
☐	☐ ....
☐	☐ ....

How can you use this book to improve research use within your context?

Drawing on your responses above, you might find it helpful to look back to the overall structure of the book (Table 1.2) and think about which chapters will be most relevant for your current context and improvement needs. You will see that there is a clear connection between the aspects of using research well listed above and the titles of the chapters listed in Table 1.2. You can therefore use your responses above as a guide for navigating this book.

For example:

If you ticked:	You might find it helpful to:
• one or a few items on the list	⇒ start with the chapter (or chapters) that relates to those aspects of using research well
• many or most items on the list	⇒ start with Chapter 2 and work your way through the book
• no items on the list	⇒ start by looking at the case study within any of the chapters to see if that stimulates any new ideas
• additional items that you added to the list	⇒ start by looking at the summary page of each chapter to see if your additional issues are covered anywhere

◉ CHAPTER REVIEW

After reading this chapter:

☐ Are you able to explain what using research well means, why it matters and how it is complex?

☐ Are you able to describe what this book provides and how to get the most out if it?

☐ Have you applied your learning to the improvement activity to identify what you want to improve and what parts of the book could help you?

☐ Have you engaged in further activities and reading in Appendix 1 to improve your understanding of using research well?

NOTES

1. All the names of educators that feature within this book are pseudonyms.
2. References are provided in each chapter's appendix. For example, see Appendix 1 for Chapter 1 references.
3. The data sources of this book are explained in the section below 'What this book is based on'.

CHAPTER 2
IDENTIFYING A CLEAR PURPOSE

USING RESEARCH WELL INVOLVES YOU:
- identifying a specific need within your setting that provides a purpose for your research use.

HAVING A CLEAR PURPOSE IS IMPORTANT BECAUSE:
- your specific need drives what research you select and how you use it.

PURPOSEFUL RESEARCH USE HELPS TO AVOID:
- focusing on external fads that are not relevant to your context; and
- improvement efforts faltering due to their rationale not being clear.

THIS CHAPTER WILL HELP YOU TO:
- identify the specific need that will drive your research use; and
- explain and promote the purpose for using research to others.

LEARN MORE ABOUT PURPOSEFUL RESEARCH USE BY:
- reading about its two key practices;
- engaging with Sascha's case study example;
- completing the improvement activity; and
- exploring Appendix 2 for further activities and reading.

INTRODUCTION

> ❝ *[My advice for using research well] would be to have a purpose – that would be number one. …You have to find something that you want to narrow in on and have a purpose. Then, it would be to set a goal for yourself in that purpose … and then it would be to actually go and find some evidence that links with what you want to do."* **(Middle leader, interview)**

To use research well, it is important that you have a clear purpose to drive what research you use and how you use it. In other words, when research is used well, it relates to a clearly identified need within your context. Quality use of research, then, does not start by looking outward to research, but rather by looking inward to your own practice and context. This chapter explores what is involved in making research use purposeful by looking inward and will be helpful if you:

- believe that research could be helpful, and want to be clear about your particular need;
- want to understand your context better using a variety of evidence and perspectives; or
- want to explain your purpose for using research to others.

There are two aspects of making research use purposeful that are important to consider. Firstly, it is important that the **research use process serves a purpose** by specifically addressing a need within your context. Secondly, it is important that you **act with purpose** when promoting and explaining the rationale for using research to your colleagues and other key stakeholders. This chapter explores these aspects of purposeful research use through two key practices:

1. specifying a need for improvement to drive your research use; and
2. promoting and explaining the purpose for using research.

These practices are important because they lay the foundation for using research well. They are the groundwork that needs to happen before you can identify appropriate research (Chapter 3) and engage with it and implement it thoughtfully (Chapters 4 and 5). These practices also help to build buy-in from colleagues by avoiding the use of research feeling ad hoc or disconnected from what matters in your context.

As you read this chapter, you might like to think about how research is used within your school or organisation and consider the following:

- Why is using research with purpose important to us?
- How could we be more purposeful in our research use?
- What need could be addressed by using research?
- How well do we explain the purpose of research use to people?
- What changes could we make to the ways in which we promote the purpose of research use?

○ KEY PRACTICE 1
SPECIFYING A NEED FOR IMPROVEMENT TO DRIVE YOUR RESEARCH USE

When educators in our work spoke about using research well, they often emphasised the need for a clear purpose (referenced in 89% of interviews, 81% of surveys). One senior leader, for example, explained that "by coming up with something that's really specific and focused ... [that's when] people are invested". This first key practice of specifying a need for improvement, then, involves:

- analysing a variety of evidence;
- considering different perspectives; and
- selecting a specific need.

ANALYSING A VARIETY OF EVIDENCE

In our work, educators stressed the importance of knowing your context and "digging deeper" (Middle leader, interview) before making any decisions about research-informed changes. A key way to achieve this understanding is by analysing various types of evidence from within your context, such as different kinds of student- and school-level data and the professional knowledge of staff (for an explanation of evidence types, see Key Concepts box in Appendix 2).

A useful starting point can be to **map out evidence sources that you are aware of and want to access, as well as any evidence that you may need to generate**. Crafting some guiding questions for yourself can help to kick-start this process. For example, one senior leader described how an existing Universal Design for Learning (UDL) framework had not been implemented consistently across her school and was not supporting teachers or students in the ways that it was intended. To determine the reasons for this situation, she described developing questions for herself that would help her to gather and consider varied evidence, and that also helped her to "narrow" in on priority needs to address:

> So, questions particularly like: Who are the people I'll go to to gather data? And how can we think beyond just quantitative data? And what's our own school report spitting out here [relative to other schools]? ... Questions that prompted the narrow focus, and drilling down to a narrowness were quite helpful."

Another step that you can take is to **make sure that your evidence can be interrogated from different angles**. For example, school-based and nationally assessed outcomes in literacy might highlight a need to improve students' results. Refining these data, let's say, by year level, student type (e.g., gender) and literacy component (e.g., reading comprehension), and then correlating with other evidence (e.g., student attendance; student engagement feedback; student outcomes in other literacy components and/or subjects) may help you to identify a particular cohort and their need for targeted attention.

Evidence over time can also be useful for highlighting trends or patterns that can provide insights into the extent or significance of a particular issue. For example, during an interview, one senior leader described how her review of trends in student attainment data and attitudinal data helped to highlight the need for significant change in the school's assessment practices:

> We weren't getting the results that we should be .... We were able to present data [to staff] – our NAPLAN data [national numeracy and literacy assessment data], our VCE [final year secondary school attainment scores], our 'attitudes to school' student survey data – all which pretty much said [that] the longer that students stayed here, the [worse the results got]. ... We had to do something different because whatever we were doing wasn't working."

CONSIDERING DIFFERENT PERSPECTIVES

As well as engaging with various types of evidence, it is also important to consider a variety of perspectives that can help you to make sense of your evidence in different ways. **Consulting or working collaboratively with colleagues and experts**, both within and/or beyond your school or organisation, is a useful strategy that can help you to do this. Table 2.1 outlines four benefits of gathering, analysing and interpreting evidence collectively with others, with illustrations of this practice provided by educators during interviews.

Table 2.1.
Benefits of consulting others to gather and analyse evidence

Benefit	Example
Minimising bias in evidence interpretation	One senior leader described the importance of working with others and listening to different perspectives to ensure a more comprehensive analysis of evidence: *" It's important that you have more than one set of eyes looking at the data. Because I think, sometimes, we can have tunnel vision depending on what it is … so, [you need to] look at it closely, drill right down to have a look at it, but do it together with colleagues so that [you're] moderating [each other]."*
Gaining deeper or new perspectives on evidence	One senior leader described her preferences for gathering evidence through professional conversations with colleagues and how these helped her to review school data through a different lens: *" I like to talk. I like lots of conversations. So, I get my [evidence] from doing a lot of qualitative discussions and then having a look at [school] data through that perspective rather than numbers. Mind you, a lot of teachers don't see it like that. … A lot of teachers are very number-based and like the data that way."*
Determining the scope of an emerging issue	One middle leader, who was seeking to implement new teaching approaches to address the impact of poverty on his students' wellbeing and learning outcomes, gathered different forms of evidence to help him understand his context better and determine the scope of the issue he was trying to address: *" I did a questionnaire [with staff] around [their] beliefs of the origins [and] implications of poverty, and how best to deal with [these]. We knew then that we would not only have to change the way teachers were working, we [would also] have to change [their] mindset."*
Broadening evidence bases by incorporating expert perspectives	One middle leader, who was determining how to improve a recently implemented synthetic phonics program that had "not had the impact we wanted", described her need to "look further afield and dig deeper" to help plan future improvements: *" I worked closely with our speech language pathologist that we employ here at school, and she does a lot of reading and searching on her speech language networks. And I've done a lot of looking through [my leadership networks] and talking to other people across the state about what's working in their schools to get some examples. … So, every time we find something … we get together, we talk about it, we share – [by now], we've sort of built up a bank of expert knowledge … [the idea is] not [about] throwing the first [phonics program] away, but just building on to it with something else."*

SELECTING A SPECIFIC NEED

At some point in the process of analysing evidence and perspectives, you will have to make a decision about which need(s) you are going to address. **Considering and responding to a number of factors** will not only help you to rank and prioritise your emerging issues, but will shape a rationale for why you are choosing to address one or more of these. Some potential considerations are suggested in Table 2.2, but these suggestions are not intended as an exhaustive list (i.e., you may have other factors that are important in your context) and are designed to be selected from (i.e., a targeted few may well be sufficient to help you select an appropriate need).

Table 2.2.
Examples of factors to consider and respond to when selecting a specific need

Colleagues' views and perspectives	Past attempts to address this need and/or use research	Feedback or input from school or organisation stakeholders	Urgency of improvement required
Alignment with school or organisational strategic goals	Type of need (e.g., improving professional knowledge vs addressing a practice issue) (Chapter 3)	A cost/effort vs risk vs impact analysis (Chapters 4 and 5)	Current workloads, schedules and capacities of staff (Chapter 5)

When selecting a need to address through research use, it is important that this need, as one senior leader explained, is "really specific and focused". In our work, educators reiterated that well-defined and specifically-articulated needs help to enable more effective searches for relevant research (Chapter 3). They also stressed that by narrowing issues, colleagues and other stakeholders were more likely to understand and support the feasibility of the intended change. **Considering and responding to some of the factors listed above may help you to define your need better.** Or you might adopt a particular technique that helps you to focus, as another senior leader, during interviews, explained:

> ❝ I try to keep [our] priorities narrow, so that we are focusing on [an issue which] links to that [school improvement plan.] … But, also, you need to choose a narrow part of [an issue]. … So, we might use some processes, like '5 Why's' to narrow it down … not make it too big."

A final aspect of your selection process is **determining how you are going to make a decision** – that is, who is going to be involved (e.g., just yourself, a small working party and/or the whole staff), the formality of the process (e.g., informal discussion and/or a formal consultation process) and the length of time over which the process will be conducted. Thinking through these elements will help with communicating your research use purpose to others, as discussed in the next key practice.

RECAP: SPECIFYING A NEED FOR IMPROVEMENT TO DRIVE YOUR RESEARCH USE

This section has outlined three ways to make your research use purposeful by identifying a specific improvement need within your context.

Specifying a need for improvement by:

analysing a variety of evidence | considering different perspectives | selecting a specific need

🔵 KEY PRACTICE 2
PROMOTING AND EXPLAINING THE PURPOSE FOR USING RESEARCH

Once you have selected the need for improvement that will drive your research use, it is important that this purpose is made clear to others within your organisation. When educators in our third survey were asked about improving the use of research, a majority (70%) indicated that it was 'important' or 'very important' that their school had 'a clear vision about research use'. To achieve this kind of clarity, the second key practice involves:

- explaining the purpose for using research; and
- promoting the purpose consistently and strategically.

EXPLAINING THE PURPOSE FOR USING RESEARCH

Using research well relies on people in your school or organisation knowing what need is driving the use of research, as well as why and how this decision was made. Again, in our third survey, most educators indicated that it was 'important' or 'very important' for leaders to 'be transparent about the source and reasons for research use' (76%), and to 'support educators' understanding of what the research means for practice' (73%). During interviews, one senior leader explained this:

> " When you want to implement something that's going to be sustainable and have a long lasting, powerful impact on student outcomes ... then you need to take your time, and you really need to explore things carefully. And you need to help your staff understand 'the why' behind the change."

Drawing on the previous section, providing people with a clear sense of purpose for research use will likely involve you **explaining information pertaining to both your decision and decision making process** (Table 2.3).

Table 2.3.
Examples of questions that will provide information to help explain the purpose of research use

What varied evidence was analysed to identify a need for improvement and why?	Who was involved in the analysis and why were those perspectives consulted?	What factors were considered in selecting the need, and how was this done?
What stakeholders will be advised of decisions and how?	Why do you believe that using research will be helpful in relation to this need?	What next steps will be taken to search for and decide on appropriate research?

PROMOTING THE PURPOSE CONSISTENTLY AND STRATEGICALLY

By making the purpose for research use clear, you will help colleagues to understand and buy in to it. Being consistent and strategic in your explanations and promotion efforts is important, as one senior school leader reflected:

> *I guess what I learned was that it's really important that everybody is on board and going in the same direction ... [there] has to be a really strategic approach to how we use research."*

Communication is therefore key – **people need to receive consistent messages about the purpose for research use**, which then flow through your school or organisation. This consistency will help to build a common and clear vision and language for research use. As one senior leader explained:

> *It comes from the top down, we have that conversation [with staff], 'This is our direction for reading [etc.]' And all that starts at the top ... that's our decision for the whole school. And it's transparent and we make sure all the staff have an understanding of what's expected ... [and we] make sure everyone gets the same message."*

It is also important that your **communication style and content are reflective of your context**. One way you can do this is by emphasising your school's or organisation's "strengths" and the relevance of these to your intended research-informed change. During interviews, for example, one senior leader shared her beliefs that connections made between the purpose of research use and "things that we're very good at" not only help to gain buy-in from colleagues, but enable a "mindset shift in wanting to be the best you can and improve".

This practice was best illustrated during an interview with one secondary school senior leader who had decided to transform the school curriculum following recommendations from a formal school review. He explained that a worthwhile purpose for using research was when it was linked "to a narrative in your context, that connects to a history or where there has been some success". He described his school as having a long history and pedagogical strength in vocational education and applied learning, and he emphasised this when explaining his ideas about "the future curriculum shape" to others:

> *I've said that this [proposed future curriculum] speaks to our strength and our history and our DNA."*

This positioning helped him to "gain the traction to get things moving" with other key stakeholders as well, such as jurisdiction leaders and parent/carer groups. He observed that by communicating in this way, "people are looking at it and just going, 'Okay, it makes sense'". Overall, this idea of "making sense" was a key success criterion of his communication and engagement campaign:

> ❝ *I'm always looking at anything that happens here [and asking], 'How do I connect it all together so it just makes sense?'"*

Finally, being consistent and strategic in your promotion also involves **enacting the purpose for research use within organisational plans** (e.g., strategic goals, performance improvement plans), **processes** (e.g., recruitment, induction, performance review) **and frameworks** (e.g., learning and assessment principles, teaching excellence rubric). Embedding research use in these ways helps to reinforce your school or organisation's commitment to and rationale for using research. Chapter 7 will take up this idea of integrating research use into school infrastructure in more detail.

RECAP: PROMOTING AND EXPLAINING THE PURPOSE FOR USING RESEARCH

This section has outlined two ways to make your research use purpose clear and understandable to others within your context.

Making your research use purpose clear to others by:

explaining the purpose for using research

promoting the purpose consistently and strategically

◎ CASE STUDY 2.1
WHAT DOES IDENTIFYING A CLEAR PURPOSE LOOK LIKE IN ACTION?

To help you to see how the two key practices discussed in this chapter can work together in action, the following case study illustrates how a secondary school leader set about making research use in her school purposeful.

Sascha is an assistant principal in a metropolitan government secondary school of average socio-economic status. During interviews, she described how she gathered and interrogated a range of evidence to help her distil the idea of developing a different student assessment model for her school.

SPECIFYING A NEED FOR IMPROVEMENT TO DRIVE RESEARCH USE

Sascha had gathered a range of evidence about student performance, wellbeing and engagement that showed how "we'd been plateauing a lot in terms of our outcomes across the board – all of our different data sets were telling us that we needed to improve". Based on the evidence gathered, as well as knowledge gained from certain academic research, Sascha "built on [a] hunch" that the summative assessment model at the school was a cause for concern:

> *I was looking at the different ways that people assess ... [and] I was looking at the grading system that we've used [in education] for 150 years that was still used [in the school]. And I knew that it was just pointless, because it wasn't resonating with kids at all. It was disengaging with kids."*

Working collectively with other leaders, she "started going down [into] more nitty-gritty detail ... starting to really look at assessment and really looking at [our] data". She commented on the importance of probing evidence deeply: "It comes back to that evidence – really being able to pinpoint [where] students [are at] with that".

She also consulted a mentor who was a principal at a different secondary school to check her understanding of what she was observing in her school, and to gain knowledge about how alternative assessment approaches might work in a similar context. She then formed an assessment working group with her school colleagues "to interrogate some of these ideas a little bit more". She commented on the benefit of these relationships and group work:

> *We all started reading a bit more ... and we started to look at how the things that we were reading about and exploring and discussing were actually put into practice and what that actually looked like at a whole-school level. And that really*

resonated. And that's about when [the decision was made to focus on assessment] and we started building our framework for our school and coming up with what that would look like."

PROMOTING AND EXPLAINING THE PURPOSE FOR USING RESEARCH

Having made the decision to design and implement a new research-informed assessment model, Sascha convened a whole-of-school presentation day prior to semester commencing to explain to staff the rationale of their decision making. One of the first things she did was to present the evidence gathered that highlighted issues with their current assessment model.

> We were able to present data [to staff] … all which pretty much said [that] the longer that students stayed here, the [worse the results got.] … We had to do something different because whatever we were doing wasn't working."

As a part of her explanation, Sascha drew on her knowledge of the school's culture, emphasising that the issue of assessment was "tangible" and relatable, and one that she believed teachers would consider as important "to look at their practice and to change their practice". She conducted a question-answer session during the presentation day to confirm that staff agreed that the issue was a priority to address.

She also emphasised to staff that it was important to "align [the research-informed initiative] with our strategic direction at the time". She commented:

> It's really important that everybody is onboard and going in the same direction. And I think … there has to be a really strategic approach to how we use research. It has to be built into what we do and how we do it. It needs to be built into our decision-making and we need to be strategically using it all of the time throughout our meeting times, the way we work at leadership, the way we work within our teaching teams, and then the way we work in our classroom."

Her explanation highlighted the risk of things continuing to be done in "adhoc" ways that "don't achieve any outcomes at all" if research use purposes and decisions were not effectively communicated and operationalised in school practices and processes. Prior to the whole-of-school presentation day, the school leadership team decided that other change initiatives would be stopped so that the assessment issue could be given full attention by staff. This led Sascha to facilitate a session with learning leaders (who would play a role down the track in helping to implement the new assessment approach) where they worked together to identify initiatives that could stop or be reconfigured to align with the strategic design of the assessment model.

Communicating this decision and the outcomes of the learning leaders' workshop at the whole-of-school presentation day helped Sascha to get buy-in to the new research-informed initiative from staff. Sascha explained that prioritising one change initiative meant that they could do it "really well":

> *I guess it's as much about being able to spotlight and do one thing and do it really well rather than trying to do everything. ... My idea was that if you come down to [the research] ... that will have such a ripple effect on everything else, that everything else will start to have an impact. And it's about taking all those [other ideas] off the table so that our entire learning area leaders team focuses."*

⊘ PUTTING THINGS INTO PRACTICE
HOW CAN I IDENTIFY A CLEAR PURPOSE?

This final section is designed to help you to move from understanding purposeful research use to enacting it within your context. The section features an improvement activity that will help you and your colleagues to identify a clear purpose for using research, and consider what you could do to improve this aspect of your work in the future.

The activity is designed in two parts:

- **Part 1** helps you identify a specific need in your school or organisation that you believe could be addressed through the use of research.
- **Part 2** introduces you to the concept of behaviours, and helps you identify actions that you can take to improve the ways that you promote the purpose of research use to others.

You can choose to complete these activity parts individually and/or with colleagues as a team.

We also encourage you to:

Look at Appendix 2 where you might like to:

- Use the practice checklist to determine how well you believe that you are currently applying the key practices outlined in this chapter and respond to the reflection prompts.
- Engage with Jason's case study about purposeful research use.
- Learn more about the key concepts used in this chapter.
- Read more about quality use of research evidence (QURE) behaviours.

Initiate a group conversation in your school or organisation about purposeful research use. This conversation might involve you comparing and discussing your responses to the improvement activity and/or your practice checklist ratings in Appendix 2. Or, as a group, you might like to discuss the reflective questions that were posed in the introduction section of this chapter.

IMPROVEMENT ACTIVITY PART 1
SPECIFYING A NEED FOR IMPROVEMENT TO DRIVE YOUR RESEARCH USE

You might already have an idea about an issue, challenge or need within your school or organisation that you believe could be addressed through the use of research.

Use the space below to describe this potential need, and then work through Steps A–C to narrow its focus and clearly specify it.

A potential need within our school or organisation that could be addressed through the use of research is:

STEP A
ANALYSE A VARIETY OF EVIDENCE

How do you know that this potential need is an issue? What evidence have you gathered that highlights this issue (e.g., NAPLAN results, student assessment data, past attempts to improve this issue that have not been effective, etc.)?

Use the template below to note each evidence type and what aspect of the need that the evidence supports.

Evidence type	How this evidence supports a particular aspect of the need

What additional evidence could you consider that you have not yet gathered? You might like to build on the list above with these evidence types in mind.

STEP B
CONSIDER DIFFERENT PERSPECTIVES

Who could you consult (either within or beyond your school or organisation) to gain different or additional perspectives that would help you to be more specific about your need?

Use the template below to note each expert and how their perspectives will benefit the specification of your need.

Expert to consult	How their perspective will benefit the specification of your need

STEP C
BRING IT TOGETHER TO CLEARLY SPECIFY A NEED TO ADDRESS THROUGH RESEARCH USE

Use the following template to clearly articulate the specific need you want to address.

Cohort (e.g., student group)	
Need	
Specific aspect(s) of the need	
Reason(s) why the need has emerged and supporting evidence	
Evidence of the need	
Scope of the need to be addressed and timeframe/ phases	
Expected outcomes	

What key factors make this specific need a priority to address?

Use the template below (listing factors from Table 2.2 in this chapter) to select and describe 1–3 factors that make your specific need a priority to address.

Factor	How this factor makes the need a priority
Colleagues' views and perspectives	
Past attempts to address this need and/or use research	
Feedback or input from school or organisation stakeholders	
Urgency of improvement required	
Alignment with school or organisational strategic goals	
Type of need (e.g., improving professional knowledge vs addressing a practice issue)	
A cost/effort vs risk vs impact analysis	
Current workloads, schedules and capacities of staff	
Note other relevant factor(s) here	

IMPROVEMENT ACTIVITY PART 2
IDENTIFYING BEHAVIOURS THAT HELP YOU PROMOTE THE PURPOSE FOR USING RESEARCH

This chapter discusses the importance of communicating consistently and strategically when promoting the purpose of research use. In this case, communicating and promoting are the key actions of interest.

Part 2 of this improvement activity will help you to improve how you communicate and promote the purpose of research through clearly articulating the specific research use behaviours or actions that you, or others, need to undertake.

WHAT IS A BEHAVIOUR?

Behaviours are observable actions – they are actions that you can see people do. When defining behaviours, a useful framework known as **ATACT** (Figure 2.1) can help you to specify who does what, when and where.

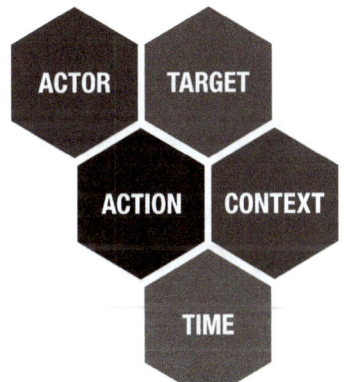

Actor: WHO performs the behaviour.
Target: WHAT is the subject of the behaviour.
Action: WHAT is done to the target item.
Context: WHERE the behaviour takes place.
Time: WHEN the behaviour takes place.

Figure 2.1. *ATACT Framework (adapted from Presseau et al., 2019)*

For example, a clearly defined behaviour regarding quality use of research could be:

> Teachers (**actor**) create a formal change plan (**action**) with at least one school-based research lead (**target**) every time (**time**) they design a new initiative (**context**)."

STEP A
PRACTISE IDENTIFYING RESEARCH USE BEHAVIOURS

Before identifying new behaviours that you can undertake yourself, you might like to practise identifying and articulating behaviours from Sascha's case study. Drawing on the ATACT Framework (Figure 2.1), an example of a behaviour that Sascha undertook to promote the purpose of research in her school was:

> " Prior to designing and implementing a new research-informed assessment model (**time**), Sascha (**actor**) convened a whole-of-school presentation day about the model's rationale (**action**) for staff (**target**) at the school (**context**)."

In this case study, there were several other behaviours that helped Sascha explain and/or promote the purpose of research use. Choose 1–2 of these actions and, using the ATACT template below, define these as behaviours. You can check your responses against answers provided in Appendix 2.

ATACT	Behaviour 1	Behaviour 2
ACTOR (Who?)		
TARGET (To what/whom?)		
ACTION (Does what?)		
CONTEXT (Where?)		
TIME (When?)		

Using the space below, you might like to write these as behavioural statements (similar to the example provided above):

STEP B
IDENTIFY YOUR OWN BEHAVIOUR TO PROMOTE THE PURPOSE OF RESEARCH USE

While Sascha is a leader in her school, taking action to promote the purpose of research use is not limited to those in formal leadership roles. Purposeful research use relies on any individual being able to clearly explain what research use looks like and why it is important, so this step aims to help you improve this aspect of your work.

Before identifying specific behaviours you would like to undertake, it can be helpful to reflect on what opportunities you have to promote the purpose of your research use within your school or organisation. Drawing on the ATACT Framework, you might like to consider some of the following prompts (Figure 2.2), with the specific need that you identified in Part 1 of this improvement activity being the reason for your intended promotion.

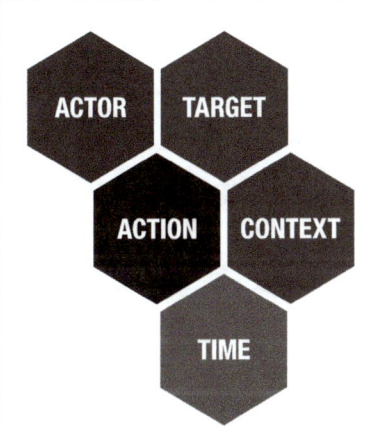

Actor: You

Target: Who needs to know the purpose? Which group(s) can you influence? Are there colleagues you need to engage so as to influence certain groups?

Action: What different opportunities and formats do you have to engage with different groups (e.g., meetings, emails. presentations, professional learning sessions, etc.)?

Context: Where might be a suitable place?

Time: When might be a suitable time? Are different groups more available/open to influence at certain times?

Figure 2.2. *ATACT Framework with promotion opportunity prompts*

You can make any notes in the space below:

....
....
....
....

After considering these prompts and drawing on the practices you have read about in this chapter, use the ATACT template below to identify 1–2 behaviours that you feel you can adopt easily that will improve the ways in which you communicate or promote the purpose of research use within your school or organisation.

For example:

> ❝ To highlight issues with our current approach to student behaviour management, I (**actor**) will present evidence regarding Year 5 student engagement (**action**) to the school leadership team (**target**) during our next monthly professional learning session (**time**) at school (**context**)."

ATACT	Behaviour 1	Behaviour 2
ACTOR (Who?)		
TARGET (To what/whom?)		
ACTION (Does what?)		
CONTEXT (Where?)		
TIME (When?)		

Using the space below, you might like to write these as behavioural statements:

To support you in making these changes, you might also want to consider and respond to the following:

- Who are you going to consult to check the feasibility of these behaviours?
- What steps are you going to take next to put these changes into action?
- When do you plan to make these changes?

◉ CHAPTER REVIEW

After reading this chapter:

☐ Are you able to describe the two key practices associated with identifying a clear purpose?

☐ Can you identify aspects of Sascha's case study that are actionable within your context?

☐ Have you applied your learning to Parts 1 and 2 of the improvement activity?

☐ Have you engaged in further activities and reading in Appendix 2 to improve your knowledge and skills regarding purposeful research use?

CHAPTER 3
SELECTING APPROPRIATE RESEARCH

USING RESEARCH WELL INVOLVES YOU:
- selecting research which is appropriate to your intended use, context, and specific improvement need.

SELECTING APPROPRIATE RESEARCH IS IMPORTANT TO:
- ensure that the research you access is trustworthy and relevant; and
- build confidence that the research will productively guide your practice.

SELECTING APPROPRIATE RESEARCH HELPS TO AVOID:
- choosing research that is inappropriate or not useful; and
- access challenges, where you cannot find what you need.

THIS CHAPTER WILL HELP YOU TO:
- determine what appropriate research means in your context; and
- carry out searches that are wide-ranging and strategic.

LEARN MORE ABOUT SELECTING APPROPRIATE RESEARCH BY:
- reading about its two key practices;
- engaging with Alex's case study example;
- completing the improvement activity; and
- exploring Appendix 3 for further activities and reading.

INTRODUCTION

> *[Appropriate research is when] the research is credible, linked to the school plan ... and [its] application in classrooms."* **(Senior leader, survey)**

To use research well, it is important that you ensure that the research you select is appropriate. In other words, the research is trustworthy but is also relevant to your context and how you intend to use it. This chapter explores what is involved when it comes to selecting appropriate research and will be helpful if you:

- wish to determine what constitutes appropriate research for your educational context;
- want guidance on how to access research that is trustworthy, contextual, and useful; or
- have a specific improvement need in mind and are now looking to find research that speaks to that focus.

Selecting appropriate research is a process that consists of two steps. It involves determining **what appropriate research means** for you in terms of trustworthiness, contextual relevance, and suitability for your intended use. Building on this first step, you then need to **access research appropriately** by thinking carefully about what you search for, where you search, and how you do so. This chapter will explore these two aspects of selecting appropriate research through two key practices:

1. determining which research is trustworthy and relevant; and
2. searching for research widely and strategically.

These two key practices are important because they help to ensure that the research you select is relevant to your purpose (building on Chapter 2). They will also set you up for success when you begin to interpret and appraise the research (Chapter 4) as well as plan how you will implement it (Chapter 5). These key practices are also valuable given the challenges that educators often face when it comes to accessing research. For example, just 36% of educators in our first survey 'agreed' or 'strongly agreed' that they could 'find research that addresses their specific practice, context, or needs'. Further, just 32% felt that they had 'sufficient access to research evidence'.

In response to these challenges, the practices discussed here will provide you with some conceptual tools and actionable strategies to help you access and navigate the research that is available.

As you read this chapter, you might like to think about how research is selected within your school or organisation and consider the following:

- How do we currently access research for our context?
- Why is it important for us to ensure that we select appropriate research?
- What sources of research are available to us that might be useful?
- How might we go about searching and selecting research in more strategic and effective ways?

◎ KEY PRACTICE 1
DETERMINING WHICH RESEARCH IS TRUSTWORTHY AND RELEVANT

Prior to beginning to look for research, it is important to take some time to think about what appropriate research means for you in your context. For the educators we worked with, this is not just a matter of appraising the quality of the research itself (referenced in 93% of interviews) but is also about considering the research in relation to how you plan to use it in your context (81% of interviews). For these reasons, this practice involves:

- understanding how you intend to use research;
- identifying important aspects of your context; and
- establishing how you will identify research that is trustworthy and useful.

UNDERSTANDING HOW YOU INTEND TO USE RESEARCH

As a first step to determining what appropriate research means for you, you need to **develop a clear picture of how you intend to use research** or, as one middle leader put it, you need to be able to answer the question, "Why would we engage with research?". Research can be used in many different ways, as illustrated in Table 3.1. So, this practice focuses on getting clear about *how* you want research to contribute to and guide your work.

Being clear about how you intend to use research is necessary because **different types of research are often better suited to particular uses**. For example, if you are looking to identify and implement a specific response to a practice challenge, then systematic reviews (such as meta-analyses which seek to statistically combine the results of multiple studies) and experimental research (such as randomised controlled trials which seek to establish causal links between interventions and impacts) are likely to be helpful for identifying impactful initiatives and implementation approaches.

Table 3.1.
Ways that research can support your practice

Use of research	Example
To develop your understanding of your practice or reflect on practice experiences	A teacher engaged with research to understand the importance of eliciting feedback from students in the classroom: ❝ Having gone through the process of [accessing research] … that's actually reinforced my own understanding of the topic, and given me, in my practice I suppose, some food for thought about how I could then alter my practice to facilitate feedback to me, … I think it's refreshed my understanding of the topic, and it's caused me to reflect on my own practice."
To identify a specific response to a practice challenge and its possible impact	When exploring how formative assessment might be enacted in her school, a senior leader turned to research to identify: ❝ Tools to be able to assess where [students] are and really understand that, and how does that look in a classroom and how does that work?"
To build buy-in or awareness about a research-informed practice change	One middle leader engaged with research to advocate for trauma-informed practices in his school: ❝ A long-term goal or long-term challenge [is] to educate teachers about the impact that trauma and poverty has on students, … and move away from the punitive measures. … The more I have my advocacy based on research, the more impact I hope to have on teacher behaviour."
To plan your implementation of a practice initiative	One middle leader used research to consider how she implemented a mentoring program at her school: ❝ [The research led to] that light bulb of, 'Oh, do we actually need to do all of these things? Or can we do things really meaningfully in a way that is going to give them the time [to participate] without taking too much of their time?'"

If, however, you are looking to reflect on and develop your understanding of the complexities of practice, you are likely to be helped more by descriptive research (which investigates a phenomenon through exploratory methods), comparative research (which investigates relationships between variables) and/or philosophical research (which uses philosophy and theory to think differently about a problem).

Furthermore, you may choose to use any of these research types to help build buy-in and awareness about a research-informed practice change. Your task, then, in thinking about your intended use of research is to **identify which research types you think will be most appropriate** (for more information on these forms of research, see Key Concepts box in Appendix 3).

You may find that you wish to lean on research in multiple ways. As one middle leader explained in an interview, they found value in using research to both enrich their understanding of a practice problem, but also to identify a possible response:

> *[The] research was helpful not just [to] fix the problem, but [also to] give us that background into why we're seeing what we're seeing ... [to] enrich our understanding and help us make a decision."*

Importantly, you will need to ensure that there is alignment between your intended use(s) of research and your specific need for improvement (as identified in Chapter 2). This will then inform the types of research you will access and how this is appropriate to your context.

IDENTIFYING IMPORTANT ASPECTS OF YOUR CONTEXT

Part of determining which research to use also involves understanding that research is not applicable to all contexts and as such, you **need to identify the contextual factors that will be important** when considering the appropriateness of certain research publications or ideas. These factors can support your decision-making, because as a senior leader explained, you can use these as a lens to evaluate the research you access:

> *It's understanding the context and part of that is the culture of the school ... and the vision and values that we work within. For us, when we're looking at any of the research that we bring into the school, we're also then putting a lens over that of 'How does this fit within what we value?'"*

While this leader's account highlights how the culture of your school may be an important factor, there are also more concrete aspects to consider. As summarised in Table 3.2, these factors may be related to your school, your staff and/or your students.

Table 3.2.
Contextual factors that may be important for appraising research

School-level factors	School sociocultural and geographical context.	School teaching and learning improvement priorities.	School vision, mission and values.
Staff-level factors	Staff research use skills, capacities and mindsets.	Staff practices and pedagogical approaches.	Staff subject disciplines and cultures of learning.
Student-level factors	Students' demographic characteristics.	Students' desired learning outcomes.	Students' academic and wellbeing needs.

When thinking about the importance of these factors, you may prefer to only use research that directly aligns with these contextual factors, as one teacher did when looking for research on writing that applied to her students:

> [I look to see] if there is a similar situational setting. So, knowing that I'm looking at students with disabilities at the moment, [I ask:] 'Is there something in there that shows me that students of 18 years of age, but working at a seven-year-old or six-year-old level, how they should be progressing, or what's the best way for writing for them?' … [Also] knowing that it'd been tested on EAL/D [English as an additional language or dialect] students made a big difference."

Alternatively, you may find that research does not directly align with every aspect of your context. In such a case, you will need to **consider what will be enough of a 'fit' between the research and your setting**. For example, one middle leader explained that he was less interested in geographical alignment than he was in the alignment of the research to his students' backgrounds and current pedagogical priorities from his Department of Education (for more on this example, see the case study later in this chapter):

> We're working in an environment of low socio-economic backgrounds. … So, we knew that, from small learning difficulties to a shortened life expectancy, we knew that the environment our students live in has a significant impact on their wellbeing and their learning outcomes … and that's where Eric Jensen's [2013] work [from America] seemed for us a plausible way of supporting students with trauma, with poverty background[s]. And this went hand in hand with the trauma-informed practice that has been an emphasis … [from our] Education Department."

The factors identified in Table 3.2 are intended as a starting point to think about the contextual aspects that are relevant for your understanding of appropriate research. Depending on your setting, there may be other factors that are important. To help identify these, there is value in collaborating with your colleagues to understand their views about the contextual factors they see as being important. In doing so, you will be better placed to consider how these factors influence what research you determine to be trustworthy and useful, as we now discuss.

ESTABLISHING HOW YOU WILL IDENTIFY RESEARCH THAT IS TRUSTWORTHY AND USEFUL

Making use of the understanding developed across the previous two sections, you can then think about what you will look for in research that might suggest it is appropriate. At the outset, it is worth emphasising the value of **working with colleagues to determine what you will look for in trustworthy and useful research**. As one senior leader explained, appropriate research "should be studied and examined carefully in a collaborative way so that it is not one person's interpretation" about what makes it trustworthy or useful.

Table 3.3.
Common markers of trustworthiness used by educators

Trustworthiness criteria	Markers to look out for
Appropriate design	Is the research design appropriate for the insights I am looking for? Is the research design appropriate for how I want to use the research?
Suitable context	Is the research context appropriate in relation to my setting? What types of students or schools were involved?
Evidence of impact	Does the research provide sufficient evidence to support the claims made?
Credible source (see also Table 3.5)	Is the author or publisher of the research reputable and credible? Did the research undergo peer review?
Recent and timely	When was the study conducted? Does it provide new and important insights?
Builds on existing knowledge	Does it build on an established research base? Is there evidence that the research contributes to a broader discussion?

With your intended use and context in mind, this practice involves **establishing a set of 'markers' of trustworthiness** you can look out for as you start accessing research. Table 3.3 summarises the kinds of criteria and markers of trustworthiness that were used by the educators involved in our work. These markers are not intended to underpin detailed appraisals of research (as will be discussed in Chapter 4) but rather to help you quickly identify research that might be trustworthy as you begin your searches.

Let us turn to some examples of this practice in action. One senior leader we worked with intended to use research to understand which reading strategies would be "most impactful for the students" and consequently, engaged with experimental types of research, such as large-scale randomised control trials, and meta-analyses of studies about different teaching strategies. In determining the trustworthiness of these types of research, he looked for markers such as whether they provided consistent evidence of impact across multiple individual trials and considered how these studies connected with the current practices in his school:

> We look[ed] for ... stuff that's been tested in trials reliably, and it's been peer reviewed, and then we often look at that and see if it's been applied in school settings as well, ... making sure it's been ... tested multiple times. ... [Then we] married it up with what [currently] happens in the classroom."

As another example, a teacher sought to use research to develop her "general concept knowledge that we have as professionals". Given her broad scope, she was less concerned with the specific types of research she was engaging with and instead focused on looking for markers that suggested the research came from a reputable source and that its insights were relevant to her students:

> So, if it's come from a source that you can trust, like if it came through the Department of Education, for example, or if it was from a university, or if it was from some reputable source where you know that they wouldn't put it there unless they had done the background research, then that can give you some confidence in using that source. … Then I would say, 'How does this actually apply to [our] students?'"

Alongside considering the trustworthiness of research, it is important to **think about what research will be accessible and useful for the staff in your school or organisation**. Often, research will not be seen as useful if it is not written in ways that resonate with the complexities of the classroom and educational practice, as a senior leader noted in an interview:

> One thing that's missing from educational research is more of the teacher's voice; written in a way that resonates with other teachers, that captures the dynamics of a classroom, the complexities of a classroom and I think that's why some educational research is not accessible by some teacher[s] because it's just not written in a way that they can see themselves relating to or connecting to [it.]"

The format in which research is published can play a large role here. For instance, while longer research formats (e.g., books) can be useful for sustained engagement with complex ideas, they have some practical challenges related to their size and the time required to engage with them. Whereas summaries or non-textual formats, such as videos and podcasts, can be useful for fostering initial discussions but can be seen as less credible and may leave out some important details in their presentation of ideas.

It is important, then, that you **identify which formats are going to be useful based on your intended use and your context**. For example, a middle leader explained how short professional journal articles provided "meeting starters" that were accessible for his colleagues:

> So generally, I'm looking for journals. So, then they're quick, sharp, and you know, we can use them as meeting starters, or just be putting out to our staff on a Friday afternoon. So generally shorter journals, … [because] I think that at the moment, in our community, we have some work to do in getting staff to use research. … [So] generally, the shorter ones are better, because I feel that the staff are more likely to engage in them."

As a guide for thinking about the forms of research that may be useful for you, Table 3.4 summarises some of the key reasons that different formats are viewed as useful (or not) by the educators in our second survey. It charts the types of research educators believed to be useful (rows) and some of the reasons why (columns).

Table 3.4.
Formats of research and why educators believe they may be useful

	Easy to apply to practice	Relevant to my practice	Easy to engage with	Credible
Practical 'how to' guides	✓	✓	✓	✓
Professional development materials	✓	✓	✓	✓
Conference materials	✓	✓	✓	✓
Short reports (<4 pages)	✓		✓	✓
Journal articles	✓	✓		✓
One-page summaries	✓	✓		✓
Books	✓	✓		✓
Book summaries	✓	✓		✓
YouTube	✓	✓	✓	
Blog posts	✓		✓	
Podcasts	✓			

Note: ✓ indicates that there was a positive relationship between the selection of a specific format (row) and the reasons for which research was considered useful (column) ($p < .05$).

RECAP: DETERMINING WHICH RESEARCH IS TRUSTWORTHY AND RELEVANT

This section has outlined three ways to select which research will be trustworthy and relevant.

Selecting appropriate research by:

understanding how you intend to use research

identifying important aspects of your context

establishing how you will identify research that is trustworthy and useful

◎ KEY PRACTICE 2
SEARCHING FOR RESEARCH WIDELY AND STRATEGICALLY

After you have thought about how you intend to use research, the types of research that will be trustworthy, and the formats that may be useful, you are now ready to begin identifying and seeking out that research. This process can be one of the most challenging aspects of using research, as you may not have a lot of experience or support with how to do it effectively and efficiently. As a result, this key practice steps through:

- looking widely for research;
- being strategic in how you conduct your searches; and
- scanning and selecting the research you will take forward.

LOOKING WIDELY FOR RESEARCH

There are multiple sources that you can use to access research that is trustworthy and useful. Each of these sources has different strengths and limitations (as detailed in Table 3.5), so **selecting research sources that align with your needs** is important. For example, one senior leader explained in an interview how they valued having access to a wide range of reliable research and, consequently, turned to academic databases:

> 🙶 *I like to actually research and read journals and access databases to you know, search for key terms, then read what's going on. That's what I like to do, and I just think that's so important, because there's a lot of studies and research that ... [you can access] that really can be helpful."*

As another example, a middle leader who worked with us wanted to find examples of research-informed practice in contexts similar to their own, so turned to the research repository hosted by their Department of Education:

> 🙶 *[Our jurisdiction has] a bank of research projects. So I could go on to that website and put in my school, size, my demographic, that sort of thing, what [topic] I was looking at. So, if I'm looking at reading for example, and it will print ... all of the projects that have been done in a similar context and on the similar subject. And then I can look at them and say, 'Well, that worked at that school.' I can contact that school, find some information, and then try and run a similar thing in our school."*

Your **search for research does not have to be a solo endeavour.** There is great value in **leveraging your professional networks** and working closely within your context (e.g., with teaching colleagues, leaders, librarians, etc.) or those you know through wider networks (e.g., social media contacts) to help you access research that is related to your

Table 3.5.
Different sources of research

Source	Strengths	Limitations	Examples
Academic databases	• Includes reliable and peer-reviewed academic publications. • Contains extensive indexing of studies across many topics. • Offers advanced search functions.	• Requires specific skills to navigate and identify relevant results. • Access is often restricted to subscribers.	• EBSCO • ERIC • Informit A+ Education • JSTOR • ProQuest
Research repositories	• Can help to identify publications related to specific contexts. • Often includes supporting practice resources.	• Requires specific skills to navigate and identify relevant results. • May not offer a broad selection of content. • Trustworthiness may be difficult to determine. • Access may be restricted.	Universities: • Monash Bridges • QUT ePrints • Melbourne Minerva Jurisdictions: • QLD Research Inventory • MACS Research Register • NSW CESE Library Research organisations: • ACER eSearch
Evidence hubs	• Focuses on practical resources that synthesise and translate a broader evidence base. • Often have clear quality criteria for resources. • Access is free.	• Advanced search functions are not common and can lead to less effective searches. • Topics are often selected based on the focus of the organisation	• AITSL Research Spotlights • Evidence for Learning Toolkit • AERO Practice Hub

focus. For example, one middle leader turned to their professional networks beyond their school to access research:

> *I've done a lot of looking through my head of curriculum networks, my master teacher network, and talking to other people across the state about what's working in their schools to get some examples."*

You can also **explore how different types of professional networks will help you access research.** Some educational jurisdictions, for example, provide their staff with access to academic databases. Many universities and public libraries also provide alumni or the public with access to their databases for personal use. These networks may be pre-existing or can be formed for the specific purpose of accessing research. Some schools, for example, have built relationships with researchers and consultants for the purpose of accessing appropriate research, as one senior leader explained:

> *Access to [research] can sometimes be a problem. But you can do that through your network, which is what we tend to end up doing, … once you've got that network, you can keep going back to those people and if they don't know, then they'll know someone in their research teams or universities that will be able to connect you back."*

For all the sources outlined above, it is important to add that **they will be more powerful if used in combination rather than in isolation.** As detailed in Table 3.5, different sources of research tend to provide access to different forms and types of research, which will be relevant to your efforts in different ways. Therefore, looking across them will allow you to compare research from different sources to ensure that what you are accessing is most appropriate for your focus.

BEING STRATEGIC IN HOW YOU CONDUCT YOUR SEARCHES

As you begin planning for and undertaking your search for literature, being strategic in your approach will set you up for success in finding research that is appropriate. As one teacher explained, this is about establishing "a clear starting point" to structure your search efforts.

A key process in this respect is to **establish a set of keywords for your searches.** Often, research publications on the same broader topic will use different keywords depending on the specific focus of the study (e.g., a mathematics paper could use keywords such as "numeracy", "division" or "secondary school mathematics"). You should define three to four keywords and any relevant synonyms that capture your focus. You can do this yourself or using an educational research thesaurus, such as the ERIC Thesaurus.

With your keywords defined, you should then spend some time **exploring the search functions of your chosen sources to help you narrow your focus** so, as one senior leader explained, "[You're] not just sitting down and saying, 'Let me just generally research.' It needs to be focused and targeted because we are time poor and there are all these other things we're doing". Some sources, for example, will allow you to apply specific subject filters, search within certain timeframes, or may even provide search tips to best navigate the platform (e.g., ERIC Search Tips).

Many academic sources will also offer an advanced search function to allow you to **prepare search strings that combine your keywords with specific search operators** (see Table 3.6). Using these features, where they are available, will allow you to be more strategic and targeted in your searches.

Table 3.6.
Operators and how they can be used in search strings

Operator	Function	Example
AND	Narrows searches by including both specified keywords	division AND multiplication AND algebra
OR	Widens searches by including at least one specified keyword	numeracy OR mathematics
NOT	Narrows searches by excluding keywords	addition NOT subtraction
*	Returns variations of a keyword	math* returns maths, mathematics, etc.
" "	Returns matches to exact phrases	"secondary school maths"
( )	Groups keywords in nested searches	(algebra AND multiplication) NOT (primary OR division)

Furthermore, you can be strategic in your searches by **introducing keywords or filters related to the type of research you are looking for**. If, for example, you are looking to develop a broad understanding of a topic that has been researched widely, including the keyword "review" in your search string will often return review articles that synthesise the findings of several previous research studies. This strategy can save a substantial amount of time and effort by quickly identifying relevant publications, as one senior leader explained when reflecting on how she accessed research with her guidance officer:

> I'd asked my guidance officer, 'Would she be actually able to go into the [database] ... and seek out actual research?' She was able to then find a literature review ... and she had pulled out bits from that literature review which she was able to present and she was able to tell us that this was peer-reviewed and those kinds of things."

SCANNING AND SELECTING THE RESEARCH YOU WILL TAKE FORWARD

It is worth noting that even with using the strategies above to target your searches, it is likely you will be presented with more research than you need. It can be tempting just to take the first few results, but these may not always be the most relevant and useful. Consequently, as a senior leader explained, it is important that you **engage thoroughly with the results of your searches and identify which are most suitable**:

> I think you've actually got to keep searching. I think like our kids, too many adults ... [look at] the first page, and they stop there. ... Don't just [take] the first page or the first book or the first article you come across. ... You need to [engage with] a body of research."

As it is not feasible to engage deeply with every research publication you come across, it is important to **develop a reading strategy that will allow you to quickly scan and get a sense of the research publication**. You may read specific sections of a publication, such as the abstract (which provides an overview of the article) or the conclusion (which summarises the key points), to evaluate whether a publication is worth saving to read in more depth later. Working as a team to collectively scan the publications you access can also help you to navigate these in a time-efficient manner.

As you are scanning a piece of research, make an **initial appraisal about whether you think it is appropriate.** This thinking process requires you to assess the research against your criteria for appropriateness (such as your important contextual factors and markers of trustworthiness as identified in Key Practice 1). As a middle leader explained:

> *I go by credibility, so [I consider] if I believe that who I am reading is credible ... I'm a historian by background, so I search and I reference my sources. And obviously it's not that [you read them] once ... I have to have a look if that has been discussed and favourably viewed by several people, so I cross reference."*

In making these initial appraisals, you are looking to **identify and earmark the research publications you believe warrant further engagement** (as will be discussed in Chapter 4). This may involve categorising or 'bucketing' them (i.e., using a 'Yes', 'No', 'Maybe' system).

Yet, in doing so, you should aim to **keep an open mind** about how the research may contribute to your practice. When scanning the research, you may come across publications that challenge your understanding as opposed to affirming it. Rather than excluding these publications, you could consider if they may enable you to make decisions from a more well-rounded perspective, as one senior leader aimed to do:

> *We tend to focus on readings that support [our understanding initially] and then we try and read things that are against it and see what the differing views are. ... We're not just looking at reading things to back up what we found ... we also try to read the other side as well."*

In other words, it is important that you are selective in the research you choose and ensure that it is relevant to your intended use, context, and improvement efforts. You also want to avoid hasty judgements based on your initial interpretations, especially when the research challenges rather than supports your point of view. This approach was described by a senior leader as "keep[ing] an open mind ... to not jump so quickly in[to] agreeing or disagreeing with evidence".

RECAP: SEARCHING FOR RESEARCH WIDELY AND STRATEGICALLY

This section has outlined three ways to carry out searches that are wide-ranging and strategic.

Searching for research appropriately by:

looking widely for research   **being strategic in how you conduct your searches**   **scanning the research and selecting what to take forward**

🔍 CASE STUDY 3.1
WHAT DOES SELECTING APPROPRIATE RESEARCH LOOK LIKE IN ACTION?

To help illustrate the two key practices discussed in this chapter in action, the following case study explores how a specialist primary school teacher for students with disabilities went about finding appropriate research.

Alex is a specialist teacher for students with disabilities at a small government primary school in an area experiencing disadvantage. During interviews, he explained how he searched for and selected research that would be appropriate to his students' needs, his colleagues' research use capacities, and the complexities of his context.

DETERMINING WHICH RESEARCH IS TRUSTWORTHY AND RELEVANT

Aware that many of his students had experienced trauma and adverse childhood experiences, Alex was looking to find research that would provide both conceptual insights into, and specific approaches for, fostering a more supportive and responsive learning environment:

> We knew that, from small learning difficulties to a shortened life expectancy, we knew that the environment our students live in has got a significant impact on their wellbeing and their learning outcomes. ... [We] knew that unless we cater the way we work to the needs of our students, we will not achieve [the] outcomes that we want to achieve."

Alex recognised that "choosing the right research is at the heart" of using it well, and as such, had three key points for determining which research would align with his efforts. First, it needed to resonate with the fact that he was "working in an environment of low socio-economic backgrounds". Second, it would need to come from a "trustworthy institution" or "trustworthy website". Third, it would have to be useful for his intended purpose of "creating awareness within [the] teaching team to use those [trauma-informed] strategies".

> I was looking for objective advice on how effective certain practices were that I was using with my students. ... We needed to make sure that we weren't just following the latest fad and actually did our homework to understand how well-researched certain practices were."

Bringing these points together, Alex was able to narrow down his understanding of what appropriate research entailed. He decided that a research-informed book represented the ideal form of research for his initiative, because it would provide in-depth background information while also unpacking different strategies that teachers could adopt in their practice:

> We did think that was important to get them some theoretical background, but we don't want to overwhelm them because they want to go on into the classroom the next day, and do something. So that's where we came into the ... [format of a] book."

ACCESSING RESEARCH APPROPRIATELY

With a clear understanding of what appropriate research meant for him, Alex started searching using multiple sources, including the "resource hub" developed by his Education Department, the suggestions of a prominent researcher in the field, and the resources of international professional associations such as the Association for Supervision and Curriculum Development. As these sources did not offer advanced search functions, he used the reference lists of the results from his initial searches to identify further resources and publications that may be relevant, which he described as doing his "homework":

> I'm doing that homework first ... [looking at the] literature, hav[ing] a look at the end [of a study]. Which studies have they used? Which books are they referring to? And then look at those books. Make your own connections, ... and then look at where the evidence [is] coming from ... and dig deeper."

As he completed these processes, Alex explained: "I'm scanning, I will [flag] ... something that I find interesting" to "focus my attention on" it later. In doing so, Alex made initial appraisals of studies against his criteria for appropriateness and trustworthiness, which allowed him to filter out studies where the "poverty aspect had not been as strong".

Through this process, Alex selected Eric Jensen's (2013) book *Engaging Students with Poverty in Mind* because he felt that it provided "a plausible way of supporting students with trauma, with poverty background[s]". Although this work was based in America, Alex felt confident in its fit because it not only aligned with pedagogical priorities from his Department of Education but also because much of the work to differentiate it to varying contexts was made clear in the book:

> Jensen's work is obviously set in the US, of course, the society is a very similar one. Plus, children's needs are, when it comes to poverty and impacts, are quite universal. And Jensen gives a toolkit for primary settings, and for secondary settings – so the differentiation was already done. So, it was only then for us to maybe do the last five or 10 per cent to really contextualise the content."

As Alex was confident in the appropriateness of the research he selected, he was able to take it forward and work with his colleagues to integrate its recommendations with their practice. This led to positive practice changes because Alex's colleagues could see the strong connection between the research, how they were using it, and their context:

> We've seen the benefits of creating awareness within our teaching team to use evidence-based strategies and understand the impact of trauma and living in poverty on students' academic [outcomes] and wellbeing. Certainly, we've seen that."

◐ PUTTING THINGS INTO PRACTICE
HOW CAN I SELECT APPROPRIATE RESEARCH?

In this final section, you will begin to move from understanding what appropriate research means to practising how to search for and select it in practice. This section features an improvement activity to support you and your colleagues to identify research that will be appropriate for your identified improvement need, and then carry out effective searches to access it.

The activity is designed in two parts:

- **Part 1** will lead you through defining what appropriate research means for you by identifying what you will look for in research that is trustworthy, useful and relevant to your context.
- **Part 2** steps through the processes involved in accessing research appropriately, including identifying possible sources of research, conducting searches of these, as well as scanning and selecting the research you will use.

You may complete these activity parts individually and/or with colleagues as a team, although we recommend that you complete them in the order they are presented below.

We also encourage you to:

Look at Appendix 3 where you might like to:

- Use the practice checklist to determine how well you believe that you are currently applying the key practices outlined in this chapter and respond to the reflection prompts.
- Engage with Emmanuel and Jade's and/or Genevieve's case studies about selecting appropriate research.
- Learn more about the key concepts used in this chapter.
- Read the *Q Data Insight* about how Australian educators source, appraise and use research in their practice.
- Read more about the different types of quality research.

Initiate a group conversation in your school or organisation about selecting appropriate research. This conversation might involve you working through the improvement activity together and/or your practice checklist ratings in Appendix 3. Or, as a group, you might like to discuss the reflective questions that were posed in the introduction section of this chapter.

IMPROVEMENT ACTIVITY PART 1
DETERMINE WHAT APPROPRIATE RESEARCH MEANS TO YOU

This chapter discusses the importance of accessing research that is trustworthy and relevant to your context and your intended use – in other words, that you access appropriate research.

This part of the activity will focus on determining what appropriate research means in relation to how you intend to use it. In Chapter 2, you focused on identifying a clear purpose for using research. You may wish to revisit the Chapter 2 improvement activity as you will be encouraged to draw from and build on your responses here.

STEP A
UNDERSTAND HOW YOU INTEND TO USE RESEARCH

On this occasion, why do you want to use research? What are you seeking to find out?

Use the space below to describe your intended use. Be specific about the content area that you're focused on and how it relates to your identified need for improvement from Chapter 2.

For example, if you have identified a need around Year 5 boys' engagement in numeracy, you may write: We have identified that Year 5 boys are less engaged in numeracy and this is negatively affecting their numeracy skills and outcomes. We are looking to use research to: i) understand the factors that influence boys' engagement in mathematics; and ii) explore different teaching strategies, lesson plan designs, and/or behaviour management approaches to better engage the boys in their numeracy learning.

How do you envision research supporting you to address this need?

From the list on next page, select the boxes which best describe how research will support your practice. If there are multiple, as described in Chapter 3, you can select more than one from the list and you may add any other ways that you intend to use research to the end of the list.

☐ Develop your understanding of practice or reflect on practice experiences.

☐ Identify a specific response to a practice challenge and its possible impact.

☐ Build buy-in and awareness about a research-informed practice change.

☐ Plan your approach to implementing a practice initiative.

☐ ....

☐ ....

As described in the chapter, different types of research will be able to support these efforts in different ways. Thinking about how different types of research provide different insights that can support your practice, use the table below to brainstorm what types of research might be suitable.

As you brainstorm, think about what 'markers' of trustworthiness you may look for in the research that you access. This enables you to be more targeted about the types of publications that you will select to take forward (looking back to Table 3.3 may help to get you started).

Research type	Why is it suitable?	What will you look for in trustworthy research?
For example, Experimental research	For example, Pre- and post-testing may indicate the effectiveness of different teaching strategies for engaging young boys in maths.	For example, I will look for research that: i) is from a credible source; ii) provides evidence of impact through statistical analyses of strategies; and iii) was published in the last 5 years.

STEP B
IDENTIFY WHICH CONTEXTUAL FACTORS ARE IMPORTANT

What are important aspects of your context to keep in mind when accessing research?

Use the space below to identify and reflect on the contextual factors you will consider to ensure that the research you access is suitable.

School-level factors:

What factors related to your school culture, priorities and demographics might be important for selecting research?

Staff-level factors:

What factors related to your colleagues' research use capacities could be relevant to selecting research?

Student-level factors:

What needs of your students require consideration when it comes to selecting research?

Which of these factors do you consider to be the most central to your research use?

Use the table on the next page to note the most central factors and why they are essential for thinking about what appropriate research means to you.

These factors will have important implications both for the types of research you deem to be trustworthy as well as the formats of research that will be useful for you. As such, we encourage you to use the right-hand column to think about how these factors will influence what you are looking for in the research you will select to use.

Central factors	Why is this factor important?	What will you look for in trustworthy and useful research?
For example, I work with students with disabilities.	For example, Their needs are specific, and it is important that the research we select reflects these needs.	For example, I'm going to look for research that includes students of similar backgrounds, or if not, I will think about what adaptations I might need to make (discussed in Chapter 4).
For example, My colleagues are new to using research.	For example, I don't want to overwhelm my colleagues with heavy academic texts while they are still getting used to engaging with research information.	For example, I'm going to look for research that includes visuals, has a short summary, or activity, or that could be easily turned into these.

Now that you have determined what suitable research means for your intended research use and context, you are ready to start the process of accessing research appropriately in Part 2.

IMPROVEMENT ACTIVITY PART 2
ACCESS RESEARCH APPROPRIATELY

Gaining access to research is often a significant barrier for educators in schools, so this part of the activity walks you through identifying possible sources of research, planning how you will search those sources for appropriate research, and how you will scan the research you come across.

STEP A
IDENTIFY AVENUES YOU CAN USE TO SEARCH WIDELY FOR SUITABLE RESEARCH

As you currently stand, what sources of research do you have access to? Looking back to Table 3.5 in the chapter may help to get you started.

Use the spaces below to brainstorm potential avenues you may have for accessing research. You do not have to fill all lines.

Academic Databases or Libraries
Do you have any access to academic databases or libraries that may be relevant?
-
-
-
-

Research Repositories
What repositories of appropriate organisations are you aware of?
-
-
-
-

Evidence Hubs
Are there any educational evidence hubs which might have relevant evidence or resources?
-
-
-
-

Professional Networks
Which of your professional networks (e.g., social media connections, memberships) may help to access relevant research?
-
-
-
-

Tip: Have a look at your brainstorming above, are there any gaps in the sources available to you that are important to address? If so, you might like to explore some additional avenues and fill them in above – you can use some of the examples from the chapter to get started (e.g., public or university libraries, jurisdiction access, personal connections).

As you may not have the capacity to search across every source listed above, which ones will be most feasible and useful for accessing appropriate research?

Spend some time exploring each source to get a sense of what they can offer, and use Table 3.5 in the chapter to help you prioritise two to three sources. Use the space below to document these sources and why you are prioritising them.

Tip: How might you be able to look across sources to engage with different types of information? How will different sources of research allow you to access research that meets your criteria for appropriateness? For instance, can some sources help to provide detailed background information for informing your decisions, while others can provide practical resources to share with your colleagues?

STEP B
DEVELOP YOUR SEARCH STRATEGY TO FIND APPROPRIATE RESEARCH

What is the content focus of your search? Write a single sentence that encapsulates what you wish to learn from engaging with research.

Tip: Look back to your intended use of research in Part 1 or the activity from Chapter 2 to help.

....

....

Identify the key words in this sentence and place them in the table below. For example, a sentence like "I am focusing on ways to support boys' engagement in numeracy in Year 5" includes the key words: boys, engagement, numeracy, and Year 5.

For each of the keywords you identify, what are some relevant synonyms? Note them in the table below:

Keywords	Relevant synonyms
For example, numeracy	For example, maths, mathematics, division, primary mathematics

Next, use the guidance in the chapter (especially Table 3.6) and the above table of synonyms to develop your search approach. You may need to test out and troubleshoot your search approach a few times to access research that will be most appropriate.

Some troubleshooting pointers include:

I have too many search results (i.e., my searches are too broad):

- Are there any subject, year, topic, or publication type filters that can be applied?
- Double-check the fields being searched (it is not recommended to search the full-text as this will pick up any peripheral mention of your keywords)
- Can you introduce any new keywords to narrow the focus?

I have too few search results (i.e., my searches are too narrow):

- Are there any keywords that you can remove without shifting the focus of your search?
- Are you using the correct search operators?

My results are not relevant:

- Do you need to search for research using a different source?
- Is there anyone you could check your keywords and search approach with to ensure that they are relevant and make sense?

The results are behind a paywall:

- Is the result available through another source? Can you search a research repository where the author may have posted a public version of the paper (see Table 3.5) or use a program, such as UnPaywall, that helps to search across open-access sources?
- Can you contact the author for a copy?

STEP C
START SCANNING AND SELECTING THE RESEARCH YOU ACCESS

Once you have your search results, your focus will shift to scanning and selecting papers that seem promising.

As you are scanning, keep in mind the criteria for trustworthiness and usefulness that you identified earlier in this activity (i.e., the tables at the end of both steps in Part 1). A strategy for keeping these aspects in mind is to have a list of questions to ask yourself as you scan a paper.

The list below proposes some questions based on what is discussed in the chapter. Add any others that are important to you.

1. *How could the research link to my purpose?*
2. *How might the research be useful?*
3. *In what ways is the research trustworthy?*
4. *How have different perspectives been captured in the research?*
5.
6.

As you answer these questions, you can begin to categorise the papers. Some categorisation strategies include "Yes/No/Maybe" or "Include/Exclude/Unsure".

You need to keep track of resources that seem promising and that you want to take forward into the next step of the process (discussed in the next chapter). This can be done by developing a table, like the one below, to store the details of the research publications and your reflections upon scanning them.

You can modify the columns based on the questions you are asking when scanning. Make sure to include a hyperlink to the source and download any PDFs/files to a single location.

Name	Link	Connection to purpose?	Usefulness?	Trustworthiness?	Yes/No/Maybe
.....	.....	.....	.....	.....	.....
.....	.....	.....	.....	.....	.....
.....	.....	.....	.....	.....	.....
.....	.....	.....	.....	.....	.....
.....	.....	.....	.....	.....	.....
.....	.....	.....	.....	.....	.....

Tip: If you are working in a team, create this table as a shared online spreadsheet so that everyone can contribute.

○ CHAPTER REVIEW

After reading this chapter:

- [ ] Are you able to describe the two key practices of selecting appropriate research?
- [ ] Can you identify aspects from Alex's case study that are relevant to your work?
- [ ] Have you applied your learning by completing Parts 1 and 2 of the improvement activity?
- [ ] Have you engaged further with the additional activities and reading in Appendix 3 to develop your understanding of selecting appropriate research?

CHAPTER 4
ENGAGING WITH RESEARCH THOUGHTFULLY

USING RESEARCH WELL INVOLVES YOU:
- using your professional judgement and expertise to make sense of research and determine how it may be brought into your practice.

ENGAGING WITH RESEARCH THOUGHTFULLY IS IMPORTANT BECAUSE:
- you need to be discerning about what you take from research into your practice; and
- you may be required to make adaptations to ensure that the research is well-suited to your context and purpose for using it.

ENGAGING WITH RESEARCH THOUGHTFULLY HELPS TO AVOID:
- undertaking a research-informed change without fully understanding its implications for your specific improvement need; and
- implementing a research-informed initiative that has not been well translated or contextualised to your setting.

THIS CHAPTER WILL HELP YOU TO:
- use critical thinking skills to develop a deep understanding of the research you access; and
- be thoughtful in how you contextualise and translate its recommendations to your practice.

LEARN MORE ABOUT ENGAGING WITH RESEARCH THOUGHTFULLY BY:
- reading about its two key practices;
- engaging with Tony, Bree and Richard's case study example;
- completing the improvement activity; and
- exploring Appendix 4 for further activities and reading.

DOI: 10.4324/9781003375845-4

This chapter has been made available under a CC-BY-NC-ND 4.0 license.

INTRODUCTION

> *[Thoughtful engagement with research involves] truly understanding and being able to interpret findings to then use this evidence to support the practices, changes, processes and projects you are implementing."* **(Senior leader, survey)**

This chapter discusses how engaging thoughtfully with research is important for using it well and how this practice draws on your professional expertise and judgement. In other words, thoughtful engagement involves fostering an active way of working with research so that you can think deeply and discerningly about what it might mean for your practice. This chapter will be helpful if you:

- want to explore what is involved in developing a comprehensive understanding of research;
- have selected research and are exploring how it may relate to your context; or
- are seeking to develop a research-informed change initiative in response to a specific improvement need.

In this chapter, we focus on two dimensions of thoughtful engagement with research. The first dimension involves **thinking about the research itself** to develop your interpretation and understanding of what it is presenting. The second dimension involves **thinking about how you work with the research** to develop a change initiative that takes its recommendations from the page to your practice. This chapter explores these two aspects of thoughtful engagement with research through two key practices:

1. interpreting the research and understanding its possible implications; and
2. being considered in contextualising and translating the research to your setting.

These two practices are important because research does not speak for itself, so there is a need to think deeply about what it means and be discerning about how it might relate to your specific improvement need (as discussed in Chapter 2). Building on your initial appraisals to determine that the research was appropriate (Chapter 3), these practices will set you up for success when it comes to implementing a research-informed change initiative in your setting (Chapter 5). As a result, thoughtfully engaging with research helps you move beyond working with research where it simply tells you what you need to know or do, towards you actively determining the path forward that you see as most appropriate for your practice.

As you read this chapter, you might like to think about how you engage with research within your school or organisation and consider the following:

- How do we currently go about developing our understanding of research that we come across?
- What forums or professional learning processes could provide opportunities to engage with research thoughtfully and collaboratively?
- What contextual factors might require us to adapt research findings to our setting?
- How will we decide whether a research-informed practice is suitable for our improvement needs?

◆ KEY PRACTICE 1
INTERPRETING RESEARCH AND UNDERSTANDING ITS POSSIBLE IMPLICATIONS

In our work, educators were clear about the importance of approaching research use in thoughtful ways by drawing on reflective and critical thinking skills (referenced in 96% of interviews, 70% of surveys). For many, strengthening these skills was a key development priority for using research well. In our third survey, we asked educators to rank 11 research use skills based on how much each one was a priority for their professional learning. Some of the most highly-ranked skills included: 'assessing whether research is useable' (42% ranked in their top 5), 'assessing the research for fit to context' (41%), and working 'with colleagues about adapting and/or connecting the research with context' (39%). As such, this key practice introduces the steps involved in:

- drawing on critical thinking skills to deeply understand research; and
- being reflective and discerning about how research will apply to your work.

DRAWING ON CRITICAL THINKING SKILLS TO DEEPLY UNDERSTAND RESEARCH

As you interpret the research you have selected, your aim is to build a deep understanding of what the research is claiming, what evidence supports these arguments, and its implications for your practice. For the educators we worked with, these efforts were important if they were to be confident that the research will have meaningful and useful applications to their work. For instance, one senior leader explained how understanding the philosophy and evidence behind a research-informed practice was important for ensuring that her use of it remained true to its "core":

> ❝ I think you need to understand the philosophy behind an approach to be able to implement it properly. To appreciate where it's come from, the basis behind it. So, you're able to ... [understand the] flavour of that program or that approach, so that everything is going in the same direction. You're not bringing in your own interpretation and diverting [too much from] the core of whatever program that is."

In short, this is about asking, as a middle and a senior leader at one school put it, "What is the research saying?" and "Where's the research [evidence] that supports that?" This points to an important thinking strategy for developing your understanding of research – asking questions. In our work, educators described how they developed their understanding by **asking questions of the research publications** they were engaging with. Asking questions can help you examine different aspects of the research, such as its trustworthiness, its possible value for your work, its suitability for your context, and its connection to your purpose for using research (see Table 4.1).

Table 4.1.
Helpful questions to ask of research

	Questions about the:		
Trustworthiness	**Value**	**Suitability**	**Purpose**
❝ Well, what was the evidence base that they had for that? Do [we] actually know what the reputation is of that author?" Senior leader, interview	❝ What does it mean? ... What does this make [us] think?" Middle and senior leader, interview	❝ [How does this link to] what we are currently doing in each of our classrooms?" Teacher, interview	❝ What need does it fill? What is the purpose? ... How are we going to check if it's right for us and our students?" Teacher, survey
❝ How did we know?" Middle leader, interview	❝ Is it something that could be useful?" Teacher, interview	❝ How do we make this work [for our setting]?" Senior leader, interview	❝ How does this actually apply to [our purpose]?" Teacher, interview
❝ What led you to that conclusion?" Senior leader, interview	❝ Is this something we need to consider for our school?" Senior leader, interview	❝ Will this work for me?" Senior leader, interview	❝ What can we take from these ... [to] develop a focus?" Senior leader, interview

In developing your understanding of specific pieces of research, it can be valuable to first make sense of the research on its own, but then consider how its **insights fit with other research and your expertise**. This process connects to your efforts in searching widely for research (see Chapter 3) by building up a picture of how an individual study is part of a larger body of knowledge. For example, two senior leaders from the same school sought to engage with research to reach "the point of feeling comfortable with the research space." They described this feeling as similar to the process of reading a novel:

> *You spend the first half of the book struggling to actually get into the book, and suddenly you are into the book and you're enjoying it, and it's familiar. I think in a tangible way, it's when reading the research becomes quicker because you understand the context in which they're making their arguments.*"

The educators we worked with emphasised the importance of **taking your time to develop this deep understanding.** They often spoke about this as an "investment of time" (Teacher, survey), where they were "investing long-term for improved outcomes [and] not just a quick fix" (Senior leader, survey). These investments of time are particularly important as they will allow you to confidently determine if a research-informed strategy is suitable for you, as a middle leader explained: "We needed to make sure that we weren't just following the latest fad and actually did our homework to understand how well-researched certain practices were."

In doing so, the educators in our work were clear that investing their time to understand the research deeply at the initial stages of a research-informed change set them up for success and allowed them to work more efficiently in the long run. As one senior leader explained:

> *Because we live in this fast-paced way that we work and schools are busy places, I think maybe that concept of slowing down to then help you speed up is something that … we might need to do a little bit more of. … When we started using [research] … other schools around us, for example, might have gone flying ahead of us, quickly, but then would stop at a plateau. Whereas we would take a lot longer to get started and then we would speed up exponentially and our outcomes would look that way too.*"

Alongside the need to take your time and ask questions of the research, consider how you might also develop your understanding of research by **working collaboratively**. This was seen as being especially useful when engaging with complex ideas or when thinking about how the research may relate to your change initiative (as will also be discussed in Chapter 5). One senior leader, for example, emphasised the value of collaboratively working with others to unpack research that was challenging to comprehend. Importantly, she did so by not only discussing the research with others, but connecting with schools who had implemented similar research-informed ideas in their contexts:

> *I think sometimes you read something and some things are so theoretical that you need to mull it over, you need to understand, you need to unpack it a little bit more by talking and seeing, experiencing [it enacted in practice]. I guess it's taking

how we learn and practising and being able to then talk about it back to somebody, and then reading it again, because then you pick up more of that detail and the nuances that you might haven't picked up on."

A useful way that you can create time to engage thoughtfully with colleagues is to **make use of existing professional learning processes**. For example, one middle leader explained how he created opportunities to unpack research by integrating a "joint book study" into his school's existing professional learning cycles: "So, the way we do it is through professional learning teams on a fortnightly cycle, where it's based on a joint book study, and we discuss strategies that are recommended in the book."

BEING REFLECTIVE AND DISCERNING ABOUT HOW RESEARCH WILL APPLY TO YOUR WORK

As you develop your understanding of what the research is saying, you can also begin to think more deeply about the relationship between the research and the specific factors of your context. These two processes may occur in tandem or can be approached sequentially, as a senior leader reflected:

> *We read through and understand [the research] at first and we sort of debrief and get our head around the main idea from the research or the body of research … then from there, we start to think about, is it something we need to consider for our school? What would it look like in the classroom? And then from there, we start to develop [our way forward]."*

This practice is about approaching the arguments of a research paper and **being open-minded and reflective** about how they may be appropriate to your work. Importantly, as we discussed in Chapter 3, the arguments of a research paper may challenge your current understanding of practice just as much as they support it. Being open-minded and reflective about these differing viewpoints, therefore, involves considering how they may collectively enable you to make more well-rounded decisions about your practice moving forward. One middle leader described this as engaging with research in a way that involves "looking widely and thinking widely about what … [your] own school [approach] will look like".

Your aim in engaging with research in this way is to **clarify the implications of the research for your work**. This will involve thinking about both the broader direction you plan to head in, as well as the specific steps that will be involved, as a senior leader explained:

> *So, I would look at those [publications] just to kind of make sure I've got a whole picture of where I'm going before I start jumping in … [as] I think you still need to be completely clear on every step along the way before you just launch in."*

The educators we have worked with spoke about certain thinking strategies being particularly useful at this point. For example, some drew on the processes involved in inquiry and action research cycles to reflect on the relationship between research and their specific improvement need. These cycles helped them to ask questions such as: What is our focus?, What do we need to know more about?, and What will we do? (see Timperley, 2012, in Appendix 4). As another example, one middle leader explained how she drew on de Bono's (1985/2017) thinking hats to consider the different ways that research publications may apply to her improvement need:

> *[My principal is] always telling me that I need to sit back and reflect and think a little bit more before I take action on things because I just like getting stuff done. And so, I read things with different perspectives. And then I tried to … do a bit of a de Bono's hats and look at things from a variety of different perspectives. … [T]hat was interesting to sort of challenge my preconceptions. It exposed me, I guess, to some new opportunities as well."*

Following this level of engagement, though, there will come a **point where you need to start making some "discerning decisions"** (Senior leader, interview) about how you will move forward. One senior leader described this as a "sticking point" where they had to determine how they would "pull together all of [their] ideas and then move … forward". In making these decisions, you should aim to be focused and "seek to do less" as you want to be "able to spotlight and do something … really well rather than trying to do everything" (Senior leader, interview). As such, you can be selective about what you take forward from a research paper, as a senior leader explained:

> *I will be looking at not taking the entire study or the entire piece of research, [but] breaking it down into smaller pieces … and working with a small part and getting that embedded in your practice before you expand it to kind of cover the whole breadth of that study."*

Importantly, there is great value in **making these decisions with your colleagues**. This may involve you generating some initial ideas which you then sense-check with your colleagues, as one teacher did:

> *[At this point, I would] consult with colleagues as well and say, 'How feasible does this sound to you?' Using the wealth of professional knowledge around me and that sort of thing to determine whether my judgments seem to be in line with those around me, because I would trust that information."*

Alternatively, you can establish more formal consultation processes. For example, one senior leader was trying to decide between "seventeen different approaches to writing" based on research. To do so, she convened a meeting of the teaching staff, which allowed them to efficiently narrow their focus and determine a way forward:

> *We put [the writing approaches] up all around the walls of a room at the school and then we came and we had a look and we asked our teachers who hadn't been part of that … [process of selecting and reading the research] to look at them all around the wall. It blew us away, straight away in the first round, that*

they said they could get rid of five approaches straight away. We said, 'Well, what was the thinking behind that?' ... [and we] unpacked that as the teaching staff. It really came back to, 'Well, this is the vision of the school, these are our values, and so therefore if we have these very strongly within us, then this is part of our consideration when we consider what we're going to use in relation to research and moving forward.'"

In considering the proposed approaches in this way, the school leader not only invited input from those who would be involved in implementing the practice change but also considered how the research aligned with their school values and context. Such information is especially useful when it comes to translating the research to your setting, which will be discussed further in the next practice.

RECAP: INTERPRETING THE RESEARCH AND ITS POSSIBLE IMPLICATIONS

This section has outlined two key practices involved in developing a deep understanding of research and its possible implications for your practice.

Engaging with research thoughtfully by:

drawing on critical thinking skills to deeply understand research

being reflective and discerning about how research will apply to your work

⬥ KEY PRACTICE 2
BEING CONSIDERED IN CONTEXTUALISING AND TRANSLATING THE RESEARCH TO YOUR SETTING

Once you have decided what you will take from the research, you can then consider how you will translate its recommendations from the page to your setting. The educators we worked with strongly emphasised the importance of being considered in how you take research forward into your practice (referenced in 96% of interviews, 83% of surveys). As such, this key practice takes you through contextualising and translating research by:

- adapting the research and connecting it to your context; and
- designing your research-informed change initiative.

ADAPTING THE RESEARCH AND CONNECTING IT TO YOUR CONTEXT

When discussing how they applied and contextualised research findings to their settings, the educators in our work emphasised that research is not just to be "picked up and used" as is (Senior leader, interview). Rather, they advocated for an active process which requires thinking deeply about what you will do with the research moving forward. Part of this active process involves **determining what adaptations, if any, you will make.** This is about ensuring that any research-informed strategies align with your setting, while remaining true to the components that are important to the original context and intent of the research. One senior leader explained that to strike this balance, you need to consider how your context is different from that of the research:

> 💬 *Don't think that what's been put in the research will work wholly in the same way in a classroom ... it might be [that you] have to make [your] own adaptations or ... the outcome will be slightly different because you've got all these variable factors that might change [from] what happened in the [original] study."*

In other words, the process of contextualising research involves **considering how you will navigate the "messiness of classroom practice"** and how you will work with research so that "it fits with all the nuances and variabilities that can happen in a classroom" (Senior leader, interview). This will be relevant even if you are working with a highly structured strategy or a research-informed program that has already been distilled and differentiated for use in an educational context. As a middle leader explained, the research they accessed provided "a toolkit for primary settings and for secondary settings – so the differentiation was already done. It was only then for us to do the last five or ten per cent to really contextualise the content."

Table 4.2.
Possible factors to consider in your adaptation of research

Factor	Example
Your students	💬 *The contextualisation is the fact of making sure that whilst we're being age appropriate, we're also at the level that the children are working at."* (Teacher, interview)
Your programs and lesson plans	💬 *You can't always have [a strategy] as your sole focus ... [so think about] the way you might approach [it in] a lesson structure."* (Senior leader, interview)
Your school processes and structures	💬 *It was developed in line with the school values and everything, and in line with our reporting structure, so that it ... had links with our school."* (Teacher, interview)
Your colleagues and school culture	💬 *You need to understand your culture and your context and your people and then you can figure out how to use that [research] in your context."* (Senior leader, interview)
Your broader priorities and agendas	💬 *We looked at literature ... and [considered how] this went hand in hand with the ... emphasis [that] has been put on by the Education Department."* (Middle leader, interview)

As you consider what will be required to contextualise the research to your setting, you may find it helpful to look back to the contextual factors that influenced your definition of appropriate research in Chapter 3. This will help you to determine if any adaptations may need to be made to the research so that it meets the needs of your programs, processes, setting, priorities, or culture (see Table 4.2).

These adaptations may also relate to how the research-informed strategy is enacted. For instance, you may choose to incorporate it into a specific program of instruction at a specific time as a way to develop and refine your existing practices and processes. You may also reframe the outcomes you expect to see, including how quickly you will achieve these outcomes and how these will be measured or evaluated. As an example, one teacher who worked in a special school explained how she adapted a research-informed reading and writing program to her students by considering: (i) the accessibility of the software she used to deliver the program; (ii) the age-appropriateness of the texts she selected; and (iii) when the program was delivered in the classroom so that her students were ready.

A helpful strategy for considering possible adaptations involves **exploring how contacts in your networks have sought to contextualise research** to their settings. For instance, one senior leader shared that when exploring how to contextualise formative assessment strategies, she used another school in her network as a "worked example":

> 💬 *They're like a worked example for us. They are like our mentor text, … we can see how that's interpreted and worked in a real-life situation, … [they've shared] what they do and how it looks …. They've been really generous, and they've shared all of their continuums of learning [to show how they have contextualised the strategies to their setting].*"

As you explore how to connect the research to your setting, it can also be valuable to **test out your intended adaptations**, especially if you are making significant changes. This may involve, for example, trialling the adapted components with one of your classes over a shorter period of time to ascertain whether they are having the outcomes that you intend. Continuing the previous example, after collaborating with the other school, the senior leader developed a formative assessment rubric for her setting. She then trialled this in her own classroom, which allowed her to make some tweaks and refinements before sharing the rubric more broadly:

> 💬 *I came home really inspired, and I came up with my own pedestrian rubric. … [Over] about four weeks I used my Year 10 class [as] a bit of a model. And it changed how I taught just in those four weeks. It really changed everything. … I think back to that Year 10 class and trialling and coming up with [my own approach] … always coming back to the classroom and testing those theories out, I think it is really important.*"

You may instead wish to undertake a larger or more formalised pilot of your adaptations to the research, in which case you will follow the detailed implementation planning approach discussed in Chapter 5. Regardless of the approach you take, in testing your adaptations, you want to make sure that you **look back to the original research** to see whether your adaptations are achieving the types of changes or outcomes that the research intended. Regularly checking back with the original research is important to ensure that your adaptations still align with the original principles and practices of the work, such that you have not introduced any "lethal mutations" (see Jones & Wiliam, 2022). The same senior leader from the previous two examples emphasised:

> 💬 *I think it's important to come back to … [our contextualised approach] in the classroom … and then coming back [to the original research] saying, 'Does it still have it?' … because it's not going to be the exact replica, so coming back and saying, 'If this is what we've come up with, is that still honouring [the research]?'*"

DESIGNING YOUR RESEARCH-INFORMED CHANGE INITIATIVE

With an understanding of what adaptations may need to be made so that the research is relevant to your context, you can then begin to think about how you will design a research-informed change initiative to translate it from the page to your setting. This practice is about recognising that "we don't just do research, decide on something ... and [then] forget about it" (Senior leader, interview). Rather, there is a need to translate the research into practice through a scaffolded process.

As an important first step, revisit your specific improvement need or purpose for engaging with research as discussed in Chapter 2. This will help you to **form a rationale that will guide your development of the research-informed change initiative.** A key component of this rationale involves connecting:

i. how your change initiative addresses an important need for improvement;
ii. your reasons for selecting this particular initiative; and
iii. the research you have engaged with to underpin these decisions.

For example, one middle leader developed a research-informed change initiative around how to best support the "students from poverty backgrounds" in his school. His rationale centred around the contention that developing a toolkit of trauma-informed practices would enable his colleagues to address challenging behaviours in ways that were more responsive to students' experiences. With this rationale in mind, he was confident in grounding this change initiative in research from Eric Jensen (2013) because the "design, impact, scalability, and [level of] investment" required seemed to be feasible: "We looked at Jensen's ways of supporting students with trauma. His work seemed a plausible approach for us and we saw that if we implemented them with consistency and with fidelity, we would get the outcomes we wanted."

As this quote suggests, with your rationale in mind, you can then articulate the changes or outcomes you hope to achieve through your initiative. In considering these expected outcomes, you are looking to **specify what the intended outcomes are** and then **determine how you will generate evidence of these outcomes**. Again, your rationale and specific improvement need will play a key role in narrowing down these intended outcomes and possible data generation approaches. To continue the example above, the middle leader explained:

> *It's important to measure the impact. To have the baseline data and look at the effectiveness of the project, to see if there's a measurable difference. ... Our outcomes focused on teachers' behaviours. Our data clearly showed that [through the initiative we had] a massive increase in positive interactions between teachers and students. Between 2019 and 2020, we achieved a 400% increase in proactive and positive interactions, while we saw a 50% decrease in reactive or negative interactions."*

Finally, you will then need to **develop the specific strategies, actions and resources** that will comprise the key components of your initiative. Educators described this as creating "the practical ways" (Teacher, survey) in which you support your colleagues to put the research into practice and "relate it to the day-to-day life of teaching" (Teacher, survey). In this step of the process, you are "trying to distil [the research into] something

Table 4.3.
Examples of components of a research-informed change initiative

Disseminating research in varying forms	Developing a research-informed pedagogical framework	Creating professional learning sessions	Forming essential agreements for research-informed programmes
💬 [We took] a strategy and … we turned it into a little postcard [that explains] … 'Why?', this is why you would do this. And then we say 'How?', and we would just put it down to some suggested approaches a teacher might take in the classroom."	💬 We develop[ed] a scope and sequence … [as] a framework for the teachers to understand what we're delivering [and our vision] for sustaining, growing and excelling [those practices and what] that would look like."	💬 We [scaffolded] engagement … and then from there, we support them in the classroom. This is what it would look like if I'm teaching the scope and sequence we've put together and it's a continual process of supporting the teachers."	💬 [With an understanding of] the programme, … from there we develop[ed] an essential agreement, how it will be taught, what's expected, what is it expected to look like in the classroom."
(Senior leader, interview)	(Senior leader, interview)	(Senior leader, interview)	(Senior leader, interview)

that is meaningful … and then basically sharing that practice" (Senior leader, interview). Importantly, the specific strategies you choose will be determined by your engagement with the research, your understanding of the context, and your knowledge of your colleagues. To support this process, Table 4.3 summarises some of the common ways the educators we worked with created research-informed change initiatives.

In short, this process involves determining the specific 'shape and form' that your research-informed change initiative will take. In working through these aspects, your aim is to be able to **clearly articulate the initiative in terms of:**

i. what actions, strategies and processes will be involved;
ii. why you are doing it in this way; and
iii. which changes you expect to see.

These steps are important for bringing others along on the journey, for as one teacher explained, your colleagues will be more likely to support your change initiative if they "know why they are teaching in a particular way and understand the rationale behind it". Once you are clear about the design of your research-informed change initiative, you will then be able to plan, deliver, and support its implementation as discussed in the next chapter.

RECAP: BEING CONSIDERED IN CONTEXTUALISING AND EMBEDDING RESEARCH

This section has outlined two key practices involved in developing a considered approach to contextualise and embed research in your context.

Thoughtfully taking research forward into practice by:

adapting the research and connecting it to your context

designing your research-informed change initiative

CASE STUDY 4.1
WHAT DOES ENGAGING THOUGHTFULLY WITH RESEARCH LOOK LIKE IN ACTION?

To help illustrate the two key practices discussed in this chapter in action, the following case study explores how three colleagues from an online school thoughtfully engaged with research.

Tony, Bree and Richard are educators at a large school which provides virtual learning for students. Tony is the acting assistant principal, while Bree and Richard are both leading teachers. Together, they deliver a 10-week enrichment program for approximately 20 students from different schools. As part of this program, the three educators were looking to use research to explore what student engagement looked like in their context and how they could "identify a range of markers that may indicate engagement in the[ir] online high ability program".

During an interview, Tony, Bree and Richard discussed how they interpreted research to understand its possible implications before adapting and translating it into their context.

INTERPRETING RESEARCH AND UNDERSTANDING ITS POSSIBLE IMPLICATIONS

A key piece of research that Tony, Bree and Richard selected was a model of engagement from Amy Berry (2020), which presented "the idea of engagement being on a spectrum from disrupting to driving". Richard reflected that this "seemed to really resonate with us", so they looked to interpret the research and consider its possible implications by asking questions about the research and how it related to their purpose:

> *I think we [did] have quite good robust discussions about our kind of core purpose and why we're doing it and what it's based on, and ... our rationale."*

They also sought to understand how the research related to their broader expertise about working with gifted students. Bree, for example, recognised that for many gifted students, "it's important to struggle, where kids who normally have success all the time, actually need to experience [that challenge]". This helped them understand an implication of the model in that it directed them to think about how they could work in partnership with students to create challenges and build engagement:

> *One of the things that I think really leapt out at us [was] about ... students taking responsibility for their engagement as well and that it wasn't just something that teachers took responsibility for or did to the students. We don't just engage the students, but we actually engage in a partnership with them."*

Reflecting on this experience, the three educators pointed to two key aspects as underpinning their thoughtful engagement with the research. First, they emphasised how it was valuable engaging with the research together, where "bouncing ideas backwards and forwards was really helpful … [because] when you're time poor, … that sort of collaborative nature of it made it a lot more efficient". Second, they emphasised how they were open-minded about the direction that the research might take them:

> " I think that was probably an important thing … we were very open minded … [in] the fact that we didn't go the first way [we came across]."

Together, these practices allowed them to develop a deep understanding of the research and be discerning about how they took its findings forward into their practice. Because they had taken the time to interpret the research and its implications, they were confident that it was the right choice of research for their initiative. As Bree explained:

> " And so … examining it deeply as I did, … I just saw, 'Oh my goodness, you know, this has great implications for us.' I was aware that Amy Berry had also done some stuff that had been applied to distance education. … [It helped me realise], 'Oh, actually, this is a really good framework [for our initiative].'"

BEING CONSIDERED IN CONTEXTUALISING AND TRANSLATING THE RESEARCH TO YOUR SETTING

Turning their attention to how to translate the engagement model to their context, the three educators realised that "a lot of what we do is a bit different from a kind of 'normal' classroom." In thinking through what made their context different, Richard discussed the characteristics of their gifted students and how they were reflected in the engagement model:

> " Our 'gifted disruptors' could actually be 'bored potential drivers'. And that really resonated with us …. If we can work out why they are disrupting – it could be that they are bored, or the challenge level isn't right … – they could be potential drivers of engagement."

Importantly, this led the three educators to adapt the engagement model to their context by reconceptualising the continuum of engagement as a "horseshoe" instead of a "straight line" to better capture their understanding of their students. They believed that sharing this adapted model would help their colleagues to feel "empowered" to recognise students' engagement and consequently, sought to "work with our teachers to be able to identify" engagement based on their model.

In doing so, though, Bree recognised that their colleagues' research use capacities were varied:

> " Different people have different capacity to digest the research, and the idea of actually bringing it and making it understandable and digestible to your community [is important]. There will be some within the community who can actually examine it from first principles, but others will need to have it scaffolded."

For these reasons, they developed a research-informed change initiative based around their horseshoe model of engagement. They distilled and shared the research with their colleagues in both summarised and original form, and created a series of questions to support teachers to reflect on how the model might be applied in their classrooms. In doing so, the three educators "didn't mandate that they use the continuum", but supported the uptake of these resources by having professional conversations with their colleagues about how they may use the model to identify markers of engagement.

Together, these actions not only helped their colleagues to understand and see the value in the model, but importantly, invited opportunities for teachers to provide input and foster ownership over its enactment moving forward.

PUTTING THINGS INTO PRACTICE
HOW CAN I ENGAGE WITH RESEARCH THOUGHTFULLY?

In this final section, you will begin to move from understanding what thoughtful engagement with research means to enacting it in practice. This section features an improvement activity to support you to adapt the research you have selected to your context.

The activity is designed in two parts:

- **Part 1** will lead you through appraising the research for adaptation.
- **Part 2** steps through testing out and finalising your adaptations.

These processes for adapting the research then provide the foundation for you to design your broader research-informed change initiative as discussed earlier in the chapter. You may complete these activity parts individually and/or with colleagues as a team, although we recommend that you complete them in order.

We also encourage you to:

Look at Appendix 4 where you might like to:

- Use the practice checklist to determine how well you believe that you are currently applying the key practices outlined in this chapter and respond to the reflection prompts.
- Engage with Steven and the #edureading group's or Jessica's case studies about thoughtful engagement with research.
- Read more about ways of thoughtfully engaging with research.

Initiate a group conversation in your school or organisation about thoughtful engagement with research. This conversation might involve you working through the improvement activity together and/or your practice checklist ratings in Appendix 4. Or, as a group, you might like to discuss the reflective questions that were posed in the introduction section of this chapter.

IMPROVEMENT ACTIVITY PART 1
APPRAISE THE RESEARCH FOR POSSIBLE ADAPTATIONS

For this improvement activity, it is important that you have selected some research that you believe is appropriate for your practice. If you have not got some research to work with, you may wish to first engage with Chapter 3 to identify, search for, and select appropriate research.

STEP A
IDENTIFY CONNECTIONS TO YOUR WORK AND POSSIBLE NEEDS FOR ADAPTATION

As you develop your understanding of your selected research, use the table on the next page to outline its key components, how they are important to the original research, and how they may be relevant to your efforts. If you identify that there are some differences between the context of the original research and your own, this may signal that some adaptations may need to be made.

An example of how this table may be completed is provided using Tony, Bree and Richard's case study above.

Research Author and title	Research components What are the key practices, arguments, or strategies from the research?	Importance to original research How are these components important in the original context or intent of the research?	Importance to our context How do these components align with (or vary from) your intended use and context?	Need to adapt?
For example, Amy Berry (2020) – Disrupting to Driving: Exploring upper primary teachers' perspectives on student engagement.	For example, Dis/engagement can be categorised on a six-point continuum – disrupting through to driving – each with several indicators; teachers understand dis/engagement holistically and as connected to the pedagogical process.	For example, The research was conducted with upper-primary teachers in Australia; explores teachers' conceptions of engagement; has an emphasis on unpacking indicators of dis/ engagement in the classroom; acknowledges the small, non-representative sample.	For example, In our context, we work with years 5-8, the students only spend 10 weeks with us, and the program is online; our students are all high achievers; however, our intention to understand and identify markers of engagement is strongly linked to the paper.	For example, Yes, in relation to: i) online context; and ii) student population.

Tip: When considering how each key practice or strategy from the research aligns with your intended uses and your context, you might like to revisit the central factors you identified during the Improvement Activity in Chapter 3 or your specified need for improvement in Chapter 2.

STEP B
ENGAGE WITH OTHERS TO EXPLORE POSSIBLE ADAPTATIONS

There is great value in consulting others to explore how you might adapt the research, considering the components you have noted in Step A.

Use the table below to gather insights from others regarding how the research could be adapted in ways that are appropriate for your context and intended use. When considering who to engage with you may wish to think about:

- **Who has prior experience?** Who within (or beyond) your school has experience adapting research in similar contexts? How might their experiences help you adapt the research? What reflections might they have about ways to ensure your adaptations still align with the core components of the research?
- **Who will be involved in the initiative?** It is important to engage early with people who will be involved in enacting the initiative, as their insights could influence how the initiative should be designed or adapted. When and where will the initiative be used? Which colleagues will this involve or impact? What suggestions might they be able to make?

Who could you reach out to and why?	What have you learned from consulting them?

STEP C
PRIORITISE YOUR POSSIBLE ADAPTATIONS OF THE RESEARCH

Based on your initial appraisal of the need for adaptations and consultations in the steps above, use the table below to prioritise the adaptations that you believe will be most relevant and important.

For instance, which components appear to be central to effectiveness in the original context? Which components do not align well with your context? What does this mean for your need to adapt the research to fit the context of your intended use? Which components could potentially be adapted without significantly deviating from the intent and rigour of the original research?

The earlier example from Tony, Bree and Richard is continued. It builds on what is presented in the case study by not only illustrating how they adapted the shape of the continuum to their high-achieving student population but also how they may have adapted the continuum's indicators to their online context.

Component of the research	Possible adaptation	Justification for this change	Possible impact of the adaptation
What aspect are you adapting or responding to?	What specific change(s) do you intend to make?	Why is this adaptation necessary – how does it enhance contextual relevance?	What is the expected impact of the adaptation(s) on outcomes?
For example, Relevance of study findings to our online context.	For example, Will adapt the indicators to be more specific to the online context.	For example, The nature of our online engagement is different, and thus, will have different indicators.	For example, Will better describe dis/engagement in our setting, but may vary the points in the continuum.
Relevance of findings to our high-achieving student population.	Rather than viewing the continuum as linear, we will view it as a horseshoe.	High-achieving students require challenge, so this may allow us to see how disruptive students are 'bored potential drivers'.	Need to explore additional strategies for partnering with students to build engagement.

Tip: If you have a long list of possible adaptation needs, focus on a few key ones to avoid the possibility that you stray too far from the original research. Consider how you will balance the two following factors that were raised in Key Practice 2:

- **Impact on alignment with context:** *How would adapting this component aim to improve its alignment with your setting? How would the adaptation enable the research to better meet the needs of your programs, processes, priorities, or culture?*
- **Impact on the research:** *How would adapting this component impact your version of the research-informed strategy? How would the adaptation influence the original intent, principles, and practices of the research?*

IMPROVEMENT ACTIVITY PART 2
PILOT AND FINALISE ADAPTATIONS TO THE RESEARCH

STEP A
TEST YOUR ADAPTATIONS

With your prioritised adaptations in mind, use the table below to consider how you will test out your adaptations to ascertain whether they are having the impact you intended.

An example inspired by Tony, Bree, and Richard's case study has been provided. In this example, they have adapted Amy Berry's (2020) indicators of engagement to be more suitable to their online context and are testing whether these adaptations are appropriate.

Rationale What aspect of the research are you adapting? What are you seeking to understand?	For example, We are exploring the usefulness of our adapted indicators of dis/engagement for the online context. We are looking to understand if the adapted indicators help us better describe how engagement occurs in our setting.
Design What is involved in your adapted strategy/initiative?	For example, We have created revised indicators of engagement for the six forms of dis/engagement in Amy Berry's model. These are based on our experiences of teaching in our setting, and our professional knowledge of high-achieving students' learning needs.
Test When and where will you test your adaptations? Who will be involved? What is the timeframe?	For example, We will test the suitability of these indicators for identifying dis/engagement in Richard and Bree's classes. Over a three-week period, Tony will conduct six 15-minute observations in both Richard and Bree's classes. These observations will occur at different stages of the lessons to develop a holistic picture of engagement across our classes.
Learnings How will you collect feedback about the test?	For example, During each observation, Tony will use a rubric that contains our revised indicators. He will tick if they are present and write a brief explanatory note. There is space in the rubric to make notes about the indicators' appropriateness or suggest alternative indicators.
Next steps Who will be involved in reflecting on the learnings from the test? How will you check back to the research as you determine your way forward?	For example, After the observation period, Tony, Bree, and Richard will meet to discuss the results of the observations. We will check how these adaptations map back to the original six forms of dis/engagement that Amy Berry identified. We will seek to minimise any variations to the overall nature of the six forms of dis/engagement in the continuum.

STEP B
REVIEW AND ARTICULATE THE ADAPTED ASPECTS OF THE RESEARCH

First, use the space below to summarise the adaptations to the research that you tested and how these changes aim to tailor it to your context:

Second, use the space below to review the adaptations in line with the original research.

Reflecting on the original research, particularly its central components identified in Part 1, are there any risks to the intent or context of the original research? Are there any components that you need to stick closely to as you develop your broader initiative?

Third, use the space below to summarise the learnings and observed outcomes from the pilot of your adaptations to the research.

These learnings may help to inform how you design your broader research-informed change initiative (see Key Practice 2). They may also be useful for communicating the value of your research-informed change and generating buy-in from your colleagues (see Chapter 5).

....

....

....

....

....

....

Having adapted and contextualised the core components of your selected research, you are now well-placed to design your broader research-informed change initiative as discussed in this chapter. We recommend that you refer to Key Practice 2, as it provides detailed guidance and examples on how to design your initiative. However, as a quick summary, this involves first developing your rationale for your initiative in terms of:

1. how your change initiative addresses your specified need for improvement;
2. your reasons for selecting this initiative; and
3. the research you have engaged with to underpin these decisions.

Then, with your rationale in mind, you can begin to flesh out the shape and form of your initiative in terms of:

1. what changes and outcomes you hope to see, including how you will generate evidence of these outcomes;
2. what is involved, including the actions, strategies and processes you will put in place as well as any resources that need to be developed; and
3. why you are doing it in this way, including how you will communicate this approach to stakeholders.

In the next chapter, we will consider various ways you can support and promote the implementation of this broader research-informed change initiative.

◯ CHAPTER REVIEW

After reading this chapter:

☐ Are you able to describe the two key practices of engaging with research thoughtfully?

☐ Can you identify aspects from Tony, Bree and Richard's case study that you could enact in your practice?

☐ Have you applied your learning to Parts 1 and 2 of the improvement activity?

☐ Have you engaged in further activities and reading and activities in Appendix 4 to extend your knowledge and skills regarding thoughtful engagement with research?

CHAPTER 5
IMPLEMENTING RESEARCH THOUGHTFULLY

USING RESEARCH WELL INVOLVES YOU:
- preparing for, trialling and implementing your research-informed initiative in context-sensitive ways.

IMPLEMENTING RESEARCH THOUGHTFULLY IS IMPORTANT BECAUSE:
- it transforms research into practice change on the ground; and
- it enables improvements related to your specific need.

THOUGHTFUL IMPLEMENTATION OF RESEARCH HELPS TO AVOID:
- implementation being done in a way that is not suited to your context; and
- practice improvements failing to be delivered in the ways intended.

THIS CHAPTER WILL HELP YOU TO:
- prepare and plan for the implementation of your initiative; and
- effectively trial and implement the initiative.

LEARN MORE ABOUT IMPLEMENTING RESEARCH THOUGHTFULLY BY:
- reading about its two key practices;
- engaging with Dylan and Eva's case study example;
- completing the improvement activity; and
- exploring Appendix 5 for further activities and reading.

INTRODUCTION

> ❝ [Using research well means] debriefing [the research] along with colleagues after a suitable trial period and trial of other methods to gather evidence of what works or not. [It also means] implementing programs that support [trial] findings and looking at results [to see] if they are consistent with similar cohorts."
> **(Teacher, survey)**

Thoughtful implementation brings together the different aspects of the research use process that has involved you deciding on an issue to address (Chapter 2), and then finding and engaging with appropriate research (Chapters 3 and 4). Implementation is the 'action' end of this process – that is, the part that transforms research into practice improvement on the ground. This chapter explores what is involved in thoughtful implementation and will be helpful if you:

- want to introduce a research-informed change initiative in your school or organisation;
- want to understand the readiness of your colleagues for this initiative;
- are keen to engage others in the implementation process; and
- want to reflect on and evaluate implementation outcomes.

The task of thoughtful research implementation involves "thinking about, preparing for, delivering, and sustaining change" (Sharples et al., 2019, p. 5) and can be considered from two perspectives.

The first perspective, 'thinking and preparing', is about the **implementation itself being thoughtful** – that is, having a well-thought-out plan that is sensitive to your current context, and thorough in its detail. The second perspective, 'delivering and sustaining', is about **you acting thoughtfully** – that is, taking a thoughtful approach to implementation that includes effectively engaging others and learning through trial and error. In our work, a majority of educators considered this type of thoughtful approach to implementation as key to the quality use of research overall (referenced in 96% of interviews, 83% of surveys).

With these ideas in mind, this chapter explores two key practices that you can undertake in your school or organisation:

1. preparing for and planning implementation; and
2. implementing research-informed change thoughtfully.

These practices are important because without them positive change cannot occur or, if it does, is at risk of not delivering the intended outcomes. As one senior leader (survey) observed:

> [Poor research use] involves inconsistent approaches among staff ... which potentially cause conflict or confuse students and parents. There would be a lack of growth perceived by staff, resulting in the potential for greater resistance to the implementation of evidence-based [change] in the future."

As you read this chapter, you might like to think about how research is used within your school or organisation and consider the following:

- How prepared are we to undertake this research-informed initiative?
- How well do we currently implement change within our school/organisation? How do we know this?
- What changes could we make to better prepare for and implement research-informed change?
- What could we stop doing to support effective implementation of this initiative?
- What would successful implementation look like?

◆ KEY PRACTICE 1
PREPARING FOR AND PLANNING IMPLEMENTATION

Along the same lines as Chapter 2, preparing and planning well for implementation requires you to look inward to your own context first before doing anything with your research-informed initiative. This idea was emphasised by one senior leader who explained that, when preparing for implementation, it was important to "think about the context [that] you are applying [research] to" including understanding "where [you] are at as a school [and] what [you] are capable of doing to move it forward". Preparing and planning, then, involves:

- assessing your organisational readiness for change; and
- developing an implementation plan.

ASSESSING YOUR ORGANISATIONAL READINESS FOR CHANGE

If you have been following the chapters in this book, by now you would have decided on a clear research-informed initiative that you are going to implement and possibly formulated some ideas about how you might go about applying it in practice. Before you can determine your implementation approach, though, an important first step is to understand and assess how ready your school or organisation is to undertake this change.

Table 5.1 illustrates a simple threefold way to think about **the readiness of your organisation to implement a research-informed initiative**. This framing is based on the premise that: Implementation Readiness = Motivation + General Capacity + Initiative-specific Capacity (Scaccia et al., 2015; Sharples et al., 2019). It shows how implementation readiness needs to be assessed in terms of:

- the motivation of the people who will be involved in the implementation;
- the nature of the organisation in which the implementation will happen; and
- and the specific requirements of the initiative that will be implemented.

Table 5.1.
Three aspects of implementation readiness

Motivation	General Capacity	Specific Capacity
❝ How motivated are people to implement this change?"	❝ What organisational capacity do we have to implement this change?"	❝ What initiative-specific capacity do we have to implement this change?"
• People's motivation towards the initiative • People's engagement with the initiative • Perceived benefits of the initiative • Compatibility of the initiative with organisational culture	• Current staffing levels and capacity • Current workload levels • Current leadership structures and capacity • Current administrative capacity • Current organisational culture and priorities	• Skills and knowledge to implement the initiative • Professional learning and coaching support • Technology, materials and resource support • Administrative and leadership support • Evaluation processes

Thinking about these aspects of readiness can be helpful not only for large-scale initiatives, such as the introduction of a new whole-school program, but also for small-scale initiatives, such as the trialling of a new strategy in one teacher's classroom.

The importance of each of these three aspects of implementation readiness was highlighted by educators during our research.

In relation to motivation, for example, there was a strong emphasis on understanding staff "change fatigue" (Middle leader, interview) as a potential threat to effective implementation. Educators described change fatigue as a cultural malaise brought about by too many and/or changing work demands. One middle leader described how excessive and poorly implemented initiatives had affected colleagues' mindsets about the value of research-informed change:

> *I definitely think staff at this school are experiencing change fatigue. There has been a number of different initiatives rolled out that have not taken hold and then not really made an impact and, so, we've got some long serving staff here who have seen these different [initiatives] - almost fads - come and go. I think the mindset is [now] that [any research-informed change] is just another one of those things - that research is an add-on, and that after we tick this box, we can get back to the real teaching."*

In connection to general capacity, a key theme highlighted was the time needed to implement and sustain practice improvements. Several middle and senior leaders spoke about "slowing things down" and "taking your time" to implement initiatives effectively. In one example, a senior leader explained that "trying to sustain and implement the use of [research-informed] practice can be really challenging when you've got a lot of competing demands". She described how she had factored longer implementation periods into her planning - "carefully, slowly building" the research use skills and interest of her teaching staff. "Perseverance" was a key aim of her planning. She concluded:

> *I would say that only in the last 18 months do I genuinely feel I've got teachers valuing research in education, to the point that I'm now thinking ... this can become even more effective in practice."*

Finally, in relation to specific capacity, a key issue that was emphasised was paying attention to colleagues' current skill levels to understand and apply the research-informed initiative in practice. Educators warned about making assumptions that colleagues would be able to use research well with little support, or be able to implement the research-informed initiative without time for trial and error. During interviews, this point was illustrated by one senior leader who realised that she "just expect[ed]" her staff to know how to adapt their practices and had not, therefore, factored the need or taken the time to "up-skill" staff in research use. She went on to describe what she would do differently to ensure better implementation of research-informed initiatives in the future:

> *I think [a barrier to implementation] is a lack of actually up-skilling. I think it's making the assumption that as a four-year trained teacher, a university graduate, you should be able to do it, and they can't ... I think if we up-skilled them, they would certainly come on board ... [and if I] give them time to [use] their research as a group, [we would] see if they can get interested and take it further."*

DEVELOPING AN IMPLEMENTATION PLAN

Following an assessment of your organisational readiness for change, you are now ready to develop a plan for how you are going to implement the research-informed practice or initiative. The key here is to recognise that the implementation of research-informed initiatives is not just about the evidence, it is also about the people who will be engaging with the evidence and how they are supported to use it in their practice. As one teacher in our work explained:

> *It's all very well to read about [the research-informed initiative] ... but often it's hard to translate that into a classroom scenario or into practice. So, having a proper plan about how to implement it in actual practice [is important]."*

While there is no set way to plan for implementation, recent years have seen the publication of several guides on the topic for educators (see Appendix 5). Drawing on these, as well as our own work, Table 5.2 **outlines an implementation planning template that you might like to follow**. It reminds us that it is helpful to delineate between:

- the initiative – that is, what you are going to do and how you are going to measure its impact (see Chapter 4); and
- the implementation – that is, the process that you are going to follow to put your initiative in place and how you are going to evaluate that process.

Table 5.2.
Implementation plan outline

Element	Activities/Considerations
The Initiative	
Problem (Chapter 2) *"Why are we implementing change?"*	• Define and articulate the priority issues you are trying to address
Initiative (Chapters 3 & 4) *"What are we going to implement?"*	• Define and articulate the research-informed initiative and any adaptations made • List the key activities of the initiative and any impacts on existing approaches
Impact (Chapters 3 & 4) *"How are we measuring initiative impact?"*	• Define and articulate the expected outcomes of the initiative and how to measure them • Consider impacts on research use capacity and practices

(Continued)

Table 5.2. *(Continued)*
Implementation plan outline

The Implementation	
Implementation Process "*How* are we going to implement?"	Implementation needs to be considered in the light of your organisational readiness assessment (see Key Practice 1). You can think about implementation planning in terms of scope, style and actions. • Define and articulate the implementation scope (e.g., target participants, key stakeholders, timeframe/phases) • Define and articulate the implementation style (e.g., consultation processes, leadership practices, communication approach) • Define and articulate the implementation actions (e.g., training/ coaching, materials/resourcing, support structures/processes, budget, monitoring/evaluation)
Implementation Outcomes "*How* are we measuring implementation process effectiveness?"	Define and articulate what outcomes are expected from implementation and how these outcomes are going to be measured. For example: • fidelity (i.e., initiative implemented as intended?) • acceptability (i.e, participants engaged and found the change appropriate?) • reach (i.e., initiative reached target cohorts as intended?) • feasibility (i.e, participants found initiative easy to apply?) • costs (i.e., budget vs actual implementation costs?) • risk mitigation (i.e., identified risks were managed?) • delivery (i.e., implementation went as planned?)

RECAP: PREPARING FOR AND PLANNING IMPLEMENTATION

This section has outlined two aspects of getting ready for implementation.

Engaging with research thoughtfully by:

assessing your organisational readiness for change

developing an implementation plan

◆ KEY PRACTICE 2
IMPLEMENTING RESEARCH-INFORMED CHANGE THOUGHTFULLY

In our work, educators emphasised the importance of acting thoughtfully when implementing a research-informed initiative (referenced in 93% of interviews). In particular, educators connected thoughtfulness with collaborative approaches to implementation that encouraged staff to experiment while being questioning, critical and reflective of new practices and change. Implementing research well, then, involves:

- conducting implementation trials; and
- engaging others in the implementation process.

CONDUCTING IMPLEMENTATION TRIALS

Trials involve "trying out" (Senior leader, interview) **a research-informed initiative first before it is implemented and integrated into practice more widely.** Trialling was viewed by educators as a key contributing factor to effective implementation overall and an important way in which to collectively engage staff in a new research-informed initiative. As one teacher observed:

> *[Successful] implementation involves debriefing along with colleagues after a suitable trial period and trial of other methods to gather evidence of what works or not.*

For the educators in our work, trials could be smaller in terms of scale (e.g., trying out an initiative in one class with one teacher), smaller in terms of scope (e.g., trying out one aspect of an initiative), and/or smaller in terms of time (e.g., trying out an initiative over a shortened time period).

Trials can be used for three main reasons:

- to look back to the research – as discussed in Chapter 4, making sure that any adaptations made to a research-informed practice or initiative are not only contextualised, but retain the intent or rigour of the original research;
- to look forwards to practice – to trial the research-informed initiative itself, determining whether it can be integrated into practice and deliver the change outcomes as intended; and
- to test the implementation plan – to assess the workability of the implementation plan, such as whether actions have been planned in sufficient detail and resources and time have been adequately accounted for.

Building on these different reasons, educators in our work highlighted a range of benefits that can come through trialling (Table 5.3) or "having a look and having a bit of time to have a play with [a research-informed initiative] and see how things work" (Teacher, interview).

Table 5.3.
Benefits of trialling a research-informed initiative

Benefit	Example
Confirming the appropriateness of a research-informed initiative	One senior leader described how she wanted to improve the pedagogical strategies used by teachers in her school to support diverse learner needs in the classroom. She started with a small-scale action research project to test out the appropriateness of a particular research-informed intervention regarding students' learning goals. Having gathered initial findings from both students and teachers, she determined that the initiative "looked] like it's a really good fit for us". She was then able to develop a plan to scale the initiative across the whole of the junior school.
Gaining insights into potential impacts	In the same example as above, the initial scope of expected outcomes from the action research project focused predominantly on individual teacher engagement and expertise. Yet, the "powerful consistency" across teacher practice brought about by the trial led to expanded expectations of collective practice effectiveness and efficiencies as implementation was scaled. Additionally, feedback from students far exceeded trial expectations, leading to a redefinition of student engagement and learning outcomes and what evidence of impact would be collected as implementation continued.
Gaining insights into staff readiness and needs	One senior leader spoke about the importance of trialling and the benefits of "start[ing] small ... rather than just throwing staff completely into the whole thing". As they trialled a new reading approach in their primary school, teachers were able to "implement change gradually" which allowed the senior leadership team to assess how ready everyone was to undertake the change. Trialling, she explained, allowed her and her colleagues to see "how [the new practice] will be taught, what's expected [and] what it's expected to look like in the classroom" which then helped to determine the best implementation approach, including the extent and types of professional learning required to train people.
Ongoing review and trial of new evidence-based practices	One senior leader explained that students' needs and outcomes are constantly changing. Because of this, her and her colleagues regularly review teaching approaches and initiatives to assess whether they "suit the [students]", and then trial new evidence-based practices. She described this as "an ongoing cycle of trawling what research is available and trialling something based on evidence ... [always going] back through that cycle of 'What are the current practices out there?' or 'What are the experts saying?' to see if [initiatives] are still meeting our needs or if more research has come out that defines something more or changes your thinking".

(Continued)

Table 5.3. *(Continued)*
Benefits of trialling a research-informed initiative

Benefit	Example
Refining a research informed initiative	One senior leader explained that trialling helped to examine and augment a research-informed initiative before implementing it more broadly across the school. She commented: "We have these reflective conversations the whole way through around 'What are we learning through this? What's working, what's not working and what haven't we even thought about in relation to this yet?'". Trial reflections helped her and her colleagues to "dig more deeply into an aspect of the research" to make improvements where necessary and ensure that "everyone is up to the next step [of the initiative] to move forward".

ENGAGING OTHERS IN THE IMPLEMENTATION PROCESS

Collective ways of working were viewed by educators in our work as key to using research well (referenced in 81% of interviews). In earlier chapters, we have seen how collaborating with others was important for identifying a clear purpose (Chapter 2), selecting appropriate research (Chapter 3) and engaging with research thoughtfully (Chapter 4).

What is significant for this chapter, though, is that **involving others is even more critical for implementing research thoughtfully**. That is because individuals' needs for collaboration intensify when trialling, implementing and evaluating research-informed initiatives. In our work, for example, educators talked about finding research as involving mainly light-touch, informal, networking-type processes, whereas when it came to implementing research, there was a need for more involved and structured collaboration-type processes. Educators described wanting an "equal voice" in implementation planning in order to foster "common language and approaches", "shared feedback and reflection" and "ongoing professional collective discussions". Figure 5.1 illustrates these intensifying needs as a continuum.

Building on these ideas, Table 5.4 sets out a number of issues to consider in relation to engaging others in the implementation process.

The considerations in Table 5.4 were exemplified by one teacher who was aiming to implement new coaching approaches and resources to improve colleagues' use of research in practice. He explained that implementation of an initiative will only be effective if there is a "whole-school approach and vision" that holds "meaning" for individuals. He continued that if people could not relate to the research-informed initiative or see themselves doing it, then implementation, even with collective engagement, would fail. It was imperative, from his perspective, to have teachers "involved every step of the way" in the shaping of implementation and evaluation. He also emphasised the importance of

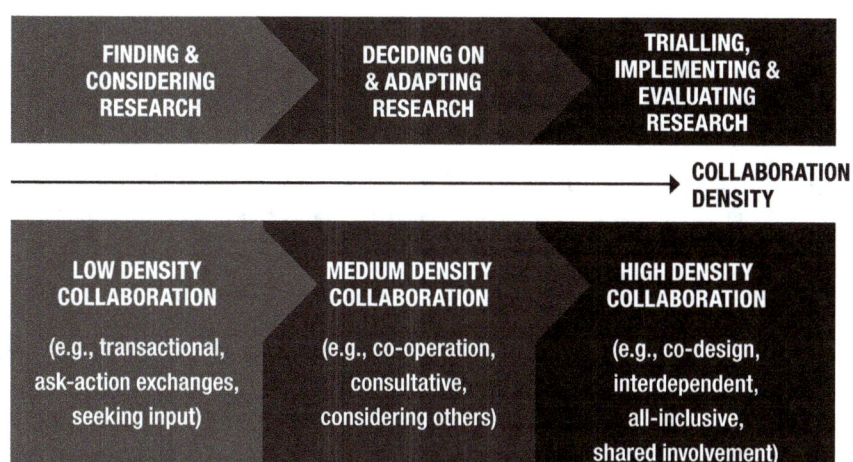

Figure 5.1. *Research use collaboration continuum*

Table 5.4.
Considerations for engaging others during implementation

	Considerations	Benefits
Building shared meaning	• How are people being engaged in defining and making meaning of the initiative? • To what extent do people have a vested interest in making the initiative work? How will this be monitored and discussed?	Avoiding superficial compliance
Involving varied voices	• Who is being involved in co-designing the implementation goals and outcomes? • To what extent do people have an equal voice? How will this be monitored and collectively discussed?	Avoiding staff disengagement
Shaping collective plans	• How are people being involved in developing the implementation approach and outcomes? • How are people being involved in translating the initiative into supporting processes and resources?	Avoiding inconsistent implementation
Tracking change over time	• How will changes in people's perspectives be accounted for during implementation? • How will these changes be incorporated into implementation plans and approaches?	Avoiding static implementation

contextualised collaboration where there was shared accountability for implementation goal setting, explaining that "[feeling] overwhelmed is probably the biggest barrier" to teachers' use of research, so leaders "have to take [that] away … and just bring it to something that can be used". Summarising, he stated:

> *I need to roll out a plan, but I need to make it meaningful for the teachers that are going to do it. Because otherwise, you just get compliance. And that's not the goal – we're trying to improve best practice which benefits students."*

RECAP: IMPLEMENTING RESEARCH-INFORMED CHANGE THOUGHTFULLY

This section has outlined two aspects of implementing research well.

Implementing research-informed change thoughtfully by:

conducting implementation trials

engaging others in the implementation process

⊙ CASE STUDY 5.1
WHAT DOES THOUGHTFUL IMPLEMENTATION LOOK LIKE IN ACTION?

To help you see how the two key practices discussed in this chapter can work together in action, the following case study illustrates how they were visible in one P-12 special school.

Dylan and Eva are the principal and deputy principal of a regional low socio-economic P-12 special school. Through their participation in a research use professional learning course, Dylan and Eva looked to implement a research-informed initiative focused on improving the school's existing team-teaching model.

PREPARING FOR AND PLANNING IMPLEMENTATION

As a part of their organisational readiness assessment and preparation for implementation, Dylan and Eva first reflected on their previous experiences of implementing research-informed changes. This process helped them to recognise the importance of ensuring the appropriateness of initiatives before implementing them. As Dylan explained:

> *Some of the things we've heard and done [before], we probably would do differently because a lot of it was aimed at mainstream [schools] and we'd have to adapt it. So now we try to look for [initiatives] that [focus on] special schools."*

These types of insights helped them to consider their selected research-informed initiative in light of their school's current priorities, capacities and organisational culture. In particular, they were keen to understand and determine how they could engage teachers, students and parents better in the implementation process than they had in the past. They gathered evidence about the current team-teaching model from these groups and sought ideas about implementation.

Teachers, for example, wanted more structured support in team-teaching and were "excited about the [proposed change]". This motivation and openness to change was an important foundation for implementation planning. Preparation also saw Dylan and Eva consulting research to determine different materials and resources that could support successful implementation and scaffold teachers' specific-initiative capacities, including "podcasts, executive summaries [of the research-informed initiative], and little Power-Point presentations".

To bring teachers into the implementation planning process, Dylan and Eva shared their own professional learning journey which they believed was "really important" to demonstrate that they were "actually investing in [their] own learning and making sure that what [they were] implementing [would work], [but] at the same time, bringing in [teachers'] perspectives". They also wanted to assure them that "we wouldn't go bang" – that change would be planned and undertaken differently than in the past: "listening to their feedback on that journey … [and] that we're not going to just bombard them with too much".

IMPLEMENTING RESEARCH-INFORMED CHANGE THOUGHTFULLY

Reflecting on learnings from past implementation experience and their own research use professional development, Dylan and Eva decided to trial their initiative as a small-scale pilot first. This was beneficial for a number of reasons. Firstly, the trial allowed them to gain feedback from participating teachers and make adjustments to both the initiative and the implementation plan. It also improved their confidence as leaders, as Dylan commented:

> The skills we've learned … we're going to bring those into the wider implementation process. … We're confident now for when we go into the mass rollout."

By trialling first, Dylan and Eva were able to provide themselves and their colleagues with sufficient time to engage properly with the research-informed initiative. Scheduled opportunities during work hours to "discuss things further and to ask each other questions" also helped to build buy-in to the initiative: "bringing people along and just drip feeding, not making it sound too big. Just one step at a time". Dylan and Eva both acknowledged that this collective engagement process was important and reflected what they had learned about their teachers and school culture through their implementation readiness assessment.

During the trial, Dylan and Eva were also able to consider how they could measure the success of the new team-teaching initiative and collect evidence of impact. Surveying all teachers about their team-teaching experiences at the beginning and the end of the year, for example, was one way that they could "have some pre- and post-data on how they're travelling". This type of data collection would not only help them to identify practice areas for improvement but also highlight what was working well during implementation and what needed to be amended. Continuous professional reflection was a key behaviour that they wanted to model to others and embed in the school infrastructure going forward. They also believed that such reflection would help them accommodate changes to implementation plans in the future:

> What we learned through our research [and professional development] was at different times during the [implementation] journey, the team will look different [and] you've got to be mindful of the importance of reflection, which we've always tried to do."

Together, they believe that the ways in which they were implementing the initiative and consulting with the school community would help to strengthen the value of the team-teaching initiative once it was rolled out more broadly across their school.

◆ PUTTING THINGS INTO PRACTICE
HOW CAN I IMPLEMENT RESEARCH-INFORMED CHANGE THOUGHTFULLY?

This final section is designed to help you move from understanding thoughtful implementation as an idea to doing it in your practice. It will help you to build up a clear sense of whether and how well you implement research-informed change at present, and what you could do to improve this aspect of your work in the future.

The improvement activity is designed in two parts:

- **Part 1** helps you to identify the actions, motivations and capacities that are needed for the successful implementation of a research-informed initiative.
- **Part 2** guides you through different motivations individuals may have and helps you to explore how you could engage colleagues in your implementation plan.

You can choose to complete these activity parts individually and/or with colleagues as a team.

We also encourage you to:

Look at Appendix 5 where you might like to:

- Use the practice checklist to determine how well you believe that you are currently applying the key practices outlined in this chapter and respond to the reflection prompts.
- Engage with Tom's case study about planning and implementing a research use initiative.
- Read more about other implementation guidance resources.

Initiate a group conversation in your school or organisation about thoughtful implementation of research. This conversation might involve you comparing and discussing your responses to the improvement activity and/or your practice checklist ratings in Appendix 5. Or, as a group, you might like to discuss the reflective questions that were posed in the introduction section of this chapter.

IMPROVEMENT ACTIVITY PART 1
IDENTIFY KEY ACTIONS, MOTIVATIONS AND CAPACITY FOR THOUGHTFUL IMPLEMENTATION

This chapter discusses the importance of assessing organisational readiness for change and developing a thoughtful plan for the implementation of research in your school or organisation.

Sometimes when developing a plan, we can make assumptions about what people will or will not do and about people's motivations and capacity to undertake change. To avoid making such assumptions, it helps to explore the perspectives of those involved.

This activity will start with you articulating specific actions needed for successful implementation. You will then be guided to explore people's views of what could enable or prevent such actions. The insights gained through this process can then be used to develop an effective implementation plan.

STEP A
IDENTIFY KEY ACTIONS INVOLVED IN SUCCESSFULLY IMPLEMENTING YOUR INITIATIVE

Consider your initiative (Chapters 3 and 4) and reflect on what successful implementation of this initiative might look like. You can refer to Table 5.2 in this chapter for aspects of implementation you might like to reflect on.

When considering what successful implementation of your initiative would look like – **who** would be doing **what** actions effectively? For example, middle leaders might trial your initiative first before finalising the implementation plan. Or you might have instructional leaders demonstrating new research-informed practices in classrooms and then observing teachers implement the practices to ensure they are implementing with fidelity.

....

....

....

....

....

....

STEP B
EXPLORING ENABLERS AND BARRIERS TO SUCCESSFUL IMPLEMENTATION

This step will involve having conversations with some of the people (**who**) that you identified in Step A, in order to find out what could enable or prevent them from performing the successful implementation actions (**what**) that you also noted in Step A.

Use the template below to explore what might enable and constrain the successful implementation of your initiative. Note that only one template is provided, but you could repeat this process for different people and actions.

Questions to understand implementation enablers and barriers

Implementation actor (who): ....

Successful implementation action (what): ....

Prompts	Actor responses
Motivations What do you see as the advantages or benefits about [the action]? What do you see as the disadvantages or drawbacks about [the action]?	
Norms Who within the team, school or beyond the school would support [the action]? Who within the team, school or beyond the school would not support [the action]?	
Capabilities and opportunities On a scale of 1–10, how easy do you think it would be for you to perform [the action]? What makes [the action] easier? What makes [the action] harder?	
Suggested supports How could these challenges be addressed? What could help you?	

STEP C
IDENTIFYING IMPLICATIONS FOR YOUR IMPLEMENTATION PLAN

Drawing on actors' responses noted in Step B, this final step involves identifying the recurring themes and their implications for your implementation plan.

Use the template below to consider the implications of your discussions with key actors for the successful implementation of your initiative.

Implementation actor (who): ....

Successful implementation action (what): ....

What key insights emerged? e.g., by the people you spoke to: was something raised repeatedly; does something significant need to be avoided; or could anything interesting be leveraged?	What could these mean for your implementation plan? e.g., for successful implementation of your initiative, you may need to...?

Motivations
-
-
-
-

Norms
-
-
-
-

Capabilities and opportunities
-
-
-
-

Suggested supports
-
-
-
-

Reflecting on your list of implications above, which of these seem most important and/or easy to plan for? Use the space below to summarise steps you wish to prioritise building into your implementation plan.

....
....
....
....
....

Tip: In Chapter 7, we provide guidance on applying a behaviour change framework to address common barriers to action – that is, the EAST framework developed by the Behavioural Insights Team (Service et al., 2014). We recommend consulting this framework, which is particularly useful for identifying strategies to overcome barriers related to complexity, appeal, social support, or timing.

IMPROVEMENT ACTIVITY PART 2
IDENTIFY WAYS YOU COULD ENGAGE OTHERS IN THE IMPLEMENTATION PROCESS

In Part 1 of this improvement activity, you identified key actions involved in implementing your initiative. You also understood these from the perspective of your audience and identified key supports you could build into your implementation plan.

In Part 2, you will identify different ways you could engage others in the implementation process. To do this, we will first guide you to identify who could be engaged in the implementation process – considering different levels of interest and influence over implementation. We will then guide you to explore different ways that you could engage those with high influence over implementation in the process.

STEP A
IDENTIFY WHO TO ENGAGE IN THE IMPLEMENTATION PROCESS

A useful way of thinking about who to engage in implementation is in terms of how **interested** people are in the implementation and **how much influence** they might have over the process.

Using the template below, list different individuals or groups you could engage in the implementation process across these three different categories.

People to keep well informed	People to keep satisfied	People to contact intermittently
People with high interest, but low influence over implementation	People with low interest, but high influence over implementation	People with low interest and low influence over implementation

STEP B
ARTICULATE WAYS IN WHICH TO ENGAGE PEOPLE IN THE IMPLEMENTATION PROCESS

This chapter introduces you to the importance of collectively engaging individuals and groups in implementation, with Table 5.4 providing some useful considerations.

Considering the people that you identified for the three categories in Step A (above), how could you engage each of them in the implementation process?

People to keep well informed could be engaged by:

....

....

....

People to keep satisfied could be engaged by:

....

....

....

People to contact intermittently could be engaged by:

....

....

....

During implementation, individuals' and groups' needs for engagement might change. For example, middle leaders involved in the trials of the initiative and the finalisation of the implementation plan may require less involvement as implementation progresses and teachers take up new research-informed practices themselves.

How might you plan for changes in engagement needs during implementation? Use the space below to summarise key steps you could take, which could inform your implementation plan.

....

....

....

....

....

○ CHAPTER REVIEW

After reading this chapter:

☐ Are you able to describe the two key practices of implementing research thoughtfully?

☐ Can you identify aspects of Dylan and Eva's case study that are actionable within your context?

☐ Have you applied your learning to Parts 1 and 2 of the improvement activity?

☐ Have you engaged in further activities and reading in Appendix 5 to improve your implementation practices?

CHAPTER 6
MODELLING QUALITY RESEARCH USE

USING RESEARCH WELL INVOLVES YOU:

- 'walking the talk' by using research well yourself and making this visible to others.

MODELLING IS IMPORTANT BECAUSE:

- people need to be shown what quality research use looks like in practice and be encouraged to follow.

MODELLING QUALITY RESEARCH USE WILL HELP YOU TO AVOID:

- being perceived as 'all talk but no action' in relation to using research well; and
- people being unclear about what quality research use looks like on the ground.

THIS CHAPTER AIMS TO HELP YOU TO:

- be a role model of quality research use; and
- demonstrate using research well to others.

LEARN MORE ABOUT MODELLING QUALITY RESEARCH USE BY:

- reading about its two key practices;
- engaging with Naomi's case study example;
- completing the improvement activity; and
- exploring Appendix 6 for further activities and reading.

INTRODUCTION

> *Leaders [need to be] able to not only quote the relevant research but be able to match it with what is happening in the school and then model the application of that research to all teachers, staff and students."* **(Teacher, survey)**

Everyone plays an important role when it comes to using research well. Leaders, though, are particularly influential in building and sustaining organisational cultures in which using research well is a feature. Individuals look to leaders for cues and direction about research use and so what leaders do and how they do it will drive how often and how well research is used within a school or organisation. Without clear leadership action, getting others to use research in their practice will be a challenge.

This chapter focuses on the leadership practice of modelling quality research use or **leading research use by doing** and emphasises the need for leaders to 'walk the talk' when using and promoting research themselves. Importantly, leading research by doing is relevant not only to those in formal leadership roles but any educator who is leading an aspect of research use or research-informed improvement. This chapter will be helpful if you want to:

- improve your own research use practices;
- encourage others by role-modelling quality use behaviours; or
- promote the professional value of research within your school or organisation.

As pointed out in previous chapters, it is helpful to think about modelling in two ways. Firstly, it is about what you do yourself as **a model of quality research use** – that is, the ways in which you use research in your own practice and invest time in developing your own research use capacities. Secondly, modelling is about what you do to show others – that is, the ways in which you **visibly model quality research use**. Using research well yourself and making that visible will encourage others to follow and use research themselves.

With these two aspects of modelling research use in mind, this chapter explores two key practices that leaders of all kinds can demonstrate in their school or organisation:

1. investing time and effort in strengthening your own research use capacities; and
2. demonstrating quality research use to others.

As you read this chapter, you might like to think about how research is used within your school or organisation and consider the following:

- Why is improving our research use leadership practices important?
- How could we improve and/or leverage our research use capacities?
- How well do we currently show others how to use research well?
- What changes could we make to the ways in which we model quality research use?

◉ KEY PRACTICE 1
INVESTING TIME AND EFFORT IN STRENGTHENING YOUR OWN RESEARCH USE CAPACITIES

Before you can effectively lead and support others in their use of research, it is important that you have developed your own quality research use capacities and practices. In our work, many educators reported valuing leaders who facilitated understandings about research by role-modelling their own research use (referenced in 67% of interviews). Overall, this practice involves:

- cultivating your own research-engaged mindset;
- developing your research use skills and practices; and
- leveraging professional relationships for your improved research use.

CULTIVATING YOUR OWN RESEARCH-ENGAGED MINDSET

In our work, having a research-engaged mindset was described by educators as a foundation of quality research use. Such a mindset involved being curious and inquisitive (referenced in 78% of interviews, 64% of surveys), as well as being open-minded about the value of research use and interested in developing your own and others' professional knowledge. Educators described the importance of these attitudes in terms of helping set the tone for research use within a school or organisation.

There are several ways in which you can demonstrate your commitment to research use while cultivating your own research-engaged mindset.

Firstly, when engaging with research, **you can consult multiple and varied sources of research**, as explained in Chapters 3 and 4, so that you broaden your knowledge, challenge your thinking and consider issues from different perspectives. Such wide-ranging engagement with research helps to develop "those good learning behaviours that we try to develop in kids", as one senior leader explained during an interview: "not being accepting, being [inquisitive], being independent thinkers, asking good questions".

So, the second way in which you can cultivate your own research-engaged mindset is **to foster inquiry as a norm** within your own practice, as well as within your school or organisational culture. One excellent example of this was provided by a senior leader during an interview. She described a time when she was challenged by a staff member about her own "inquiry stance" while the school was implementing a pedagogical change initiative:

> Actually, one of my teachers said to me, 'Well, it's great, but the kids are making a shift and we're making a shift as teachers, but what about you guys as leaders? What's the shift going to be there and how are we going to visibly notice that shift in leading?' That was a big 'aha' moment for me and I thought, 'Fair call'."

The incident prompted her to reflect on her leadership practices, particularly around using research herself and promoting research use to others. She constructed "a personal narrative of experience of my career as a principal so far – reflecting on what's happened in my career along the way to get me to the point that I'm at ... where I'm ready to learn and shift my leadership and find new ways". As she planned this "shift", she read various research studies, particularly around "understanding the mindsets and dispositions that sit behind that work of inquiry" and reached out to academics in the field to improve her professional knowledge. She also shared her reflections with staff, which helped to demonstrate her openness to changing her own mindset, as well as her leadership approaches more broadly.

DEVELOPING YOUR RESEARCH USE SKILLS AND PRACTICES

As discussed in the next chapter, developmental support is critical to helping individuals improve their research use skills and increase their use of research in practice. In our work, several educators described the importance of them undertaking professional learning activities themselves, as well as ensuring that colleagues and students saw them as 'learners'.

One way of developing your research use skills, as well as your broader knowledge and leadership capacities, is **to undertake post-graduate qualifications.** During an interview, one senior leader explained how undertaking such studies, including a Master of Teaching (Leading Learning) and a Graduate Diploma in Student Wellbeing, had not only "equipped [him] so much better to be able to lead" school-based research-informed initiatives, but also improved his leadership capacities:

> I think part of authentic leadership is to take on ideas other than just your own, and while experience counts for something ... you, yourself, have to keep gathering evidence and further your understanding of what is best for students. ... I feel that if I'm not informing myself, I'm not able to do that part of my role properly."

Undertaking such qualifications may not be feasible, so **other professional learning might be more achievable**. This can be in the form of experiences external to your school or organisation, such as attending conferences that feature research and evidence use. For example, one senior leader, who participated in a research use professional development program with a group of colleagues, described during interviews the importance she placed on her own specific research use skill development and the optics of this within her own school setting:

> *As the Deputy Principal Learning and Teaching, I actually want to be doing as well as supporting. It's not okay for me to just say, 'Well, you guys go off and do [the training] and tell me about it'. So, I really wanted to be involved at that level ... and it was terrific."*

Finally, you might like **to create developmental opportunities for yourself and your colleagues** within your school or organisation. For example, you and your leadership colleagues could read case studies of research use and reflect on the applicability of these to your own situation, or use the QURE Assessment Tool[1] (bit.ly/quretool) and work through the associated tailored scaffolds (see Appendix 6 for activities that you might like to undertake). In our work, one school leadership team described doing this – utilising the tool "to have conversations about strengths and weaknesses, [that] also helped [to] identify an area that [we] wanted to work on". They went on to comment:

> *It's not often, very rarely, that leadership teams get the opportunity to reflect on the effectiveness of how they're using research. So that was ... quite novel to have time to do that."*

This type of professional learning affected the ways in which the leadership team then led improved research use within the school. The improvement area they selected focused on the research use capacity development of middle leaders, who were accountable for overseeing staff professional learning through the school's inquiry cycle processes and structures. The leadership team created a goal around this objective in their strategic plan and made sure that their own and middle leaders' individual performance plans reflected the need for improved leadership and capacity around research use.

LEVERAGING PROFESSIONAL RELATIONSHIPS FOR YOUR IMPROVED RESEARCH USE

Another way that you can develop your own research use capacity is by leveraging relationships with others. These **relationships might be with colleagues within your school or organisation who can provide you with advice about or insights from research**. A good place to start could be identifying colleagues who are undertaking professional learning or tertiary qualifications and asking them to share new ideas or knowledge with you and others. For example, during an interview, two senior leaders from one school described how colleagues who had recently completed or were undertaking post-graduate studies at the time had not only proved to be excellent sources of research but also helped to build the research use skills and capacities of the broader leadership group:

> *Usually you've got someone who's doing a post-grad[uate program] or has done a post-grad[uate program] in each office ... and I think that's created in the offices a culture of discussing best practice."*

Professional relationships with others beyond your school or organisation can also help to develop your research use skills and knowledge. As a first step, you might like to map those people you already know who could help, and then those whom you would like to approach and build a relationship. The examples in Table 6.1, which come from senior leaders during interviews, could act as prompts for considering potential sources of support. You will have an opportunity later in this chapter to reflect on your social and professional networks and identify colleagues and experts who can help you to develop your research use capacities.

Table 6.1.
Examples of external sources of support for research use

Collaborating with principal colleagues	Tapping into varied networks
One secondary school senior leader described how she reached out to a principal in another school whom she had previously shadowed during a leadership development program. She used him as a "sounding board" and a "reference point" for the design and implementation of her change initiative: firstly, reading different research herself and formulating how that could be applied in her school; and then visiting his school and talking with him to "see how [the same research had been] interpreted and worked in a real-life situation". These "check-ins" helped to build her knowledge of the research and its application in her setting.	Another senior leader in a primary school described how she "loves to network" and had built a "system" of mentors, experts and colleagues to help her access and interpret different research-informed ideas and practices. She drew on relationships with her state-based professional association and a formal network of school leaders in order to "know what's happening in other schools … to source widely, filter, and really pick out the important parts that are great for my staff, my community and my students". She also consulted regularly with an external mentor, her jurisdiction leader, and a small number of academics and experts, to say "This is what I need - can you help me with the change that I'm trying to create?"
Working with university researchers	**Partnering with a specific researcher**
Two senior leaders from another secondary school described working with researchers from a university as they implemented new teaching approaches to improve students' learning retention. The researchers helped them to access and interpret varied research. One of the leaders observed that the benefit of the relationship was that "difference … to be able to have that dialogue and to check for understanding. And often, [when] a question was asked, [the researchers] would be able to reach into their knowledge and go, 'It's not exactly that, it's actually more this. And if you wanted to explore that, well you could use this - this is the evidence for that'".	A primary school principal described her interest in the work of one particular researcher and felt that a partnership would help her and colleagues' professional development, as well as the implementation of strategic change within the school. When asked how she had formed the partnership, she responded with "I just asked … I emailed her and said 'I have a proposal for you … I've got this idea, would you be interested in working with our school? … We'd like you to come over and just see what the school is like and give us some feedback … be our critical friend'". The partnership has been maintained over several years and has helped to develop leaders' and teachers' research use capacities.

RECAP: INVESTING TIME AND EFFORT IN STRENGTHENING YOUR OWN RESEARCH USE CAPACITIES

This section has outlined three ways to develop your own research use capacities as a leader.

Being a model of quality research use yourself by:

cultivating your own research-engaged mindset

developing your research use skills and practices

leveraging professional relationships for your improved research use

🔍 KEY PRACTICE 2
DEMONSTRATING QUALITY RESEARCH USE TO OTHERS

It is important that you are aware of the impact – either positive or negative – that your own research use behaviours and practices can have on others. In our work, a majority of educators indicated that improved research use was reliant on 'leaders demonstrating and role-modelling research use and implementation' (75% rated as 'important' or 'very important' in third survey) and 'research being used to inform decision making' (74%).

Overall, demonstrating quality research use as a practice involves:

- showing others how to use research well;
- leading a knowledge sharing culture; and
- promoting the professional value of research use.

SHOWING OTHERS HOW TO USE RESEARCH WELL

Role-modelling quality research use can be done in two main ways. Firstly, building on the previous section, it is helpful to ensure not only that you engage with research yourself and invest in developing your own research use capacities, but also that **your research use attitudes and behaviours are visible to others**. In our work, educators described this as 'walking the talk' – providing important signals to others that you are prepared to enact yourself what you are asking of others, as one senior leader explained during an interview:

> 💬 *Always know that you've got to be ready for learning [any] time. I've got to model that behaviour that I want my teachers to show myself."*

Secondly, role-modelling involves **you showing others how a research-informed practice can be implemented in practice**. In our work, educators talked about the importance of demonstrating research-informed practices, for example, during professional learning sessions or within classroom lessons. One excellent example was provided by a small group of early career teachers at one primary school. They explained how, in addition to structured professional learning, they spent two hours each week with the deputy principal to learn more about certain research-informed practices that were being applied at the school. These sessions provided valuable developmental opportunities for these teachers where they were "all thinking together". One teacher went on to comment:

> 💬 *We ask as many questions as we need to and we get answers. Everyone's listening, everyone is participating. [The sessions are] really good because we can all bounce off each other."*

Role-modelling by the deputy principal and supporting the teachers with exemplar materials was also key to the effectiveness of this particular developmental program. As another teacher explained:

> [The deputy principal] was able to give us examples of what lessons would look like - she sat down and actually showed me how to program a particular lesson and I could work my way through that. And then she also came into the classroom, and she taught a lesson in front of me ... I was able to see what she was showing us in terms of the theory, and then she put it into practice for me in the classroom ... and she gave me feedback."

Chapter 7 extends these ideas of role-modelling quality research use by suggesting various organisational structures (e.g., instructional leader models) and processes (e.g., inquiry cycle processes) in which role-modelling can feature.

LEADING A KNOWLEDGE SHARING CULTURE

In our work, educators indicated that 'a culture of knowledge sharing' is an important enabler of improved research use (81% rated as 'important' or 'very important' in third survey). In addition to viewing this culture as important, most expressed wanting to be active participants in it by 'sharing knowledge about practice within the school' (63%) and 'generating new knowledge about teacher practice' (63%).

In your role, you can cultivate knowledge sharing practices in two main ways. Firstly, **you can share knowledge yourself and role-model these behaviours for others**. For example, one senior leader described how she would often share books with new teachers to help them improve their use of research:

> A lot of the time I would walk over to my bookshelf and grab a book and say, Why don't you start with this? And then that might help you synthesise what you're asking for, and then I can help you find that specific question. Or I can connect you to someone who would be able to support you with that."

Another approach to personally sharing knowledge is to curate research yourself and share it or write about a piece of research and distribute this to staff via a regular newsletter. A senior leader from a different school described the knowledge sharing practices within her leadership team:

> Our principal compiles a series of readings for us to do, probably on a fortnightly basis, which we use largely just for discussion. ... She might also set a book that has educational research as its focus, and that might be a reading that we do across the term ... and it might inform, further down the track, maybe, the development of policy or a program. Or it just informs our thinking about our approaches on a day-to-day basis in our leadership roles."

The second way in which you can promote knowledge sharing is **to formalise it within organisational processes**, such as inquiry cycles, strategic planning processes, or curriculum design forums (see Chapter 7). An excellent illustration of leveraging improvement planning processes was provided by one senior leader during an interview:

> *The expectation is that [the leaders] are developing professionally, and then they share that professional knowledge. So, we share educational readings or articles that have a link or through-line to what we're currently working on ... [each of us is] responsible for one of the key improvement strategies within our annual implementation plan or strategic plan. So, [we're] actually required to demonstrate what [we're] doing to actually shift that data or move whatever is [our] key improvement strategy. And [we] are expected to be looking at best practice ... expected to be using evidence to support that, and then sharing that with the rest of the leadership team."*

PROMOTING THE PROFESSIONAL VALUE OF RESEARCH USE

A strategy you can use to demonstrate quality research use is to acknowledge and promote the professional value of research use to others. In our work, most educators made clear that using research well had significant implications for how they understood their own professionalism (referenced in 81% of interviews). For example, when educators were asked about 'what makes research use worthwhile', most 'agreed' or 'strongly agreed' that 'it increases my professionalism' (referenced in 80% of third survey responses), and 'it empowers me and my practice' (77%).

Along the same lines as showing others how to use research, you can connect the value of research use with colleagues' professional identities in two main ways. Firstly, **you can regard research use as being a part of your own ethical obligations and professional conduct as an educator and make this acknowledgement visible**. As one senior leader explained during interviews:

> *My responsibility is to absolutely keep abreast of all educational research and to keep in touch with developments in [particular] fields and make sure that I'm using [research] to inform my own thinking about education at my school. [For example], to review and evaluate procedures and programs that we might be doing, and then also to look at future initiatives that we might engage in."*

If you take this stance, you will signal to others that research use is not just important, but a professional responsibility, and can help to shape the school or organisational culture.

Secondly, **you can promote the professional value of research use by connecting it with performance planning and review processes within your setting**. For example, one school leadership team described canvassing individuals' views about how research use could contribute to their professional conduct, and then co-creating goals that were included in school and individual performance plans. They also asked staff to self-report (on a biannual basis) the impact of research use on their professional development, which helped the leadership team to tailor research-based learning opportunities for individuals and teams.

As another example, a senior leader from a different school explained how she had connected research use with staff promotion and opportunities to take on leadership responsibilities at her school. She described how she viewed research use as a professional obligation of her staff - "[it] isn't extra work, it's actually asking [staff] to think more deeply about the work that they [already] do" – and had, therefore, integrated goals around using research and improving professional knowledge within annual performance review processes.

RECAP: DEMONSTRATING QUALITY RESEARCH USE TO OTHERS

This section has outlined three ways to demonstrate quality research use to others within your school or organisation.

Demonstrating quality research use to others by:

showing others how to use research well in their work

leading a knowledge sharing culture

promoting the professional value of research use

🔍 CASE STUDY 6.1
WHAT DOES MODELLING QUALITY RESEARCH USE LOOK LIKE IN ACTION?

To help you to see how the two key practices discussed in this chapter can work together in action, the following case study illustrates how they were visible in the work of a secondary school middle leader.

Naomi is the Head of the English Faculty in a metropolitan, average socio-economic status government secondary school. During interviews, she and the members of the English faculty described how Naomi had led trials of new teaching strategies to improve students' reading and writing.

BEING A MODEL YOURSELF

Naomi, alongside the deputy principal, Max, immersed herself in research to consider new teaching strategies. Over several months, Naomi set aside scheduled time in her diary each week to read and analyse multiple sources/types of research. From the outset, Naomi wanted to use research because she associated it with her "professional practice" as an educator. She also explained that by engaging widely with research, "we [knew] where to start. [Without it], it would have been a lot more guesswork". She went on to describe the benefits of reading research for her own knowledge, but also the ways in which she started to question the relevance of different ideas given the school context:

> ❝ [The teaching of] reading is a big area to tackle … the more that we read, the less we could see that there was actually a neat solution. So, the research has been invaluable in that the more that we dug, the more resonances that we saw across things … and now we're sort of starting to think, 'Well how does that work in our context?'"

Naomi also leveraged relationships with senior English faculty members to help build her professional knowledge. She did this by hosting weekly meetings, both in groups and one-on-one, where she and others shared different readings and checked their understanding of research with each other. During these meetings, common assessment criteria were determined so that there was a shared understanding of research-informed strategies that would "fit" their context. Naomi explained:

> ❝ [During meetings] we were certainly talking back and forth about having read something and what we picked up on. So, it affirmed that we were on the right track if we're [all] connecting with something. … We were [also] trying to decode

> [the research] and go 'What could that look like?' – so, having another voice to balance off and also to realise that we're thinking similar things. And we also synthesised a lot of the readings too, made a little synthesis table that we could see commonalities across [the strategies] as well and discount some of them pretty quickly."

Weekly team meetings with the English faculty team allowed Naomi to share what she was doing to build her research use capacities, which then encouraged others to develop their own research use mindsets, skills and relationships. Team members could see how Naomi herself was learning over time, which made it "safe" for others to experiment with research themselves. Max was reflecting on the effectiveness of Naomi's leadership when he stated:

> It's about using research [yourself] and then encouraging more teachers to be developing their expertise with research."

ROLE-MODELLING FOR OTHERS

During trials of the new teaching approach, Naomi role-modelled strategies in classrooms with teachers observing. These demonstrations were followed by debrief sessions, where teachers and leaders within the faculty discussed what worked and what didn't during implementation, and then brainstormed potential improvements. Teachers were then provided with opportunities to trial approaches themselves in classrooms, with leaders observing. This cycle of debriefing, making improvements and trialling was repeated until all English faculty team members felt confident in applying the new strategies. Andie, an early career teacher in the faculty, commented:

> Seeing those strategies ... that had been fairly new to me being modelled by a leader in the school was a great way to see how effective they could be because, you know, they aided my learning. ... It actually helps me visualise what I'm going to be learning today."

Naomi went on to reflect about her own leadership practices that contributed to successful implementation:

> I only know the way in which I ran it was that I invested my time, and I tried to lead by example. ... It was really about slowing things down. ... We did it slowly, and slowly embedded it through one program. And then when we found it worked, we went onto another program. ... And the faculty kind of led together, and as a result, they found it very empowering. And they realised how beneficial that sort of model of professional learning is."

One faculty teacher explained that the idea of "bottom-up leadership" – where "everyone in the faculty has been given some sort of leadership responsibilities by Naomi" – was a critical aspect of the trials. Through modelling, Naomi not only encouraged team members to use research but also helped them to develop their broader professional and research use leadership capacities. As Max, the deputy principal, observed:

> *Research [use] really builds leadership by building expertise and authority. So, in terms of a leadership development strategy, it's [about] creat[ing] the space and people will become more expert and have more influence [to] lead."*

Finally, Naomi modelled practices that would sustain a culture of using research within the faculty. Research use was embedded in everyday schedules and processes, and she continued to build knowledge sharing practices and research use leadership capacities on an ongoing basis with her team. Simon, another faculty teacher, observed:

> *I think modelling the success of something you've been trialling is really important. And this is where I think the way that Naomi structures our faculty meetings is also quite good … Naomi will always find time to let you showcase a moment of success or showcase some research."*

⊘ PUTTING THINGS INTO PRACTICE
HOW CAN I MODEL QUALITY RESEARCH USE?

This final section is designed to help you to move from understanding modelling quality research use to enacting it within your context. The section features an improvement activity that will help you and your colleagues to practise modelling and consider what you could do to improve this aspect of your work in the future.

The activity has three parts:

- **Part 1** builds on your knowledge of behaviours (from Chapter 2) and helps you to identify actions that you can take to improve your own research use capacities.
- **Part 2** leads you through a brainstorming exercise to help you to identify colleagues or experts, both within and beyond your school or organisation, who you could connect with to improve your research use knowledge and skills.
- **Part 3** asks you to specify current opportunities within your school or organisation where you could demonstrate to others how to use research well.

You can choose to complete these activity parts individually and/or with colleagues as a team.

We also encourage you to:

Look at Appendix 6 where you might like to:

- Use the practice checklist to determine how well you believe that you are currently applying the key practices outlined in this chapter and respond to the reflection prompts.
- Engage with Marcus' and/or Bianca's case studies that feature research use modelling practices.
- Use the QURE Assessment Tool (bit.ly/quretool) to assess your own research use capacities and access tailored scaffolds that will support your improvement.
- Read the *Q Behavioural Insight* about how to promote knowledge and research sharing practices within your school or organisation.
- Lead a *Q Conversation* about sharing research with colleagues.
- Read more about quality use of research evidence (QURE) behaviours.

Initiate a group conversation in your school or organisation about modelling quality research use. This conversation might involve you comparing and discussing your responses to the improvement activity and/or your practice checklist ratings in Appendix 6. Or, as a group, you might like to discuss the reflective questions that were posed in the introduction section of this chapter.

IMPROVEMENT ACTIVITY PART 1
INVESTING TIME AND EFFORT IN STRENGTHENING YOUR OWN RESEARCH USE CAPACITIES

This chapter discusses the importance of developing your own research use capacities. In this case, actions that develop and/or leverage your research use mindset, skills and/or relationships are the key actions of interest.

Part 1 of this improvement activity will help you to improve your research use capacities through new behaviours. Chapter 2 introduced you to behaviours and the ATACT framework. If you would like to practise identifying and articulating behaviours before applying the ATACT framework to improvements you would like to make, you can revisit the Chapter 2 improvement activity. You can also review the key behaviours Naomi performed to improve her own research use capacities (see case study in this chapter), which we've highlighted below.

WHAT BEHAVIOURS WERE PERFORMED BY NAOMI?

Naomi undertook three key actions to build her research use capacities. Using the ATACT framework, these can be articulated as behaviours as follows:

1. To improve her own research use capacities and professional knowledge, Naomi (**actor**) read and analysed (**action**) multiple sources/types of research (**target**) every week (**time**) while at school (**context**).
2. In order to check her understanding of different research/readings, Naomi (**actor**) consulted (**action**) colleagues (**target**) in weekly (**time**) meetings at school (**context**).
3. To review the relevance of different research, Naomi (**actor**) developed common assessment criteria (**action**) with colleagues (**target**) in weekly meetings (**time**) at school (**context**).

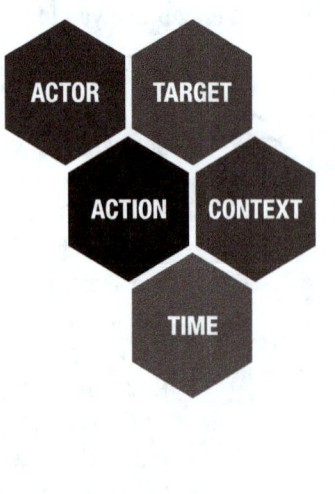

STEP A
IDENTIFY PERSONAL BENEFITS THAT CHANGE COULD BRING

Before identifying a specific behavioural change you would like to make, it can be helpful to reflect on the personal value that change in this area could have. In other words, consider **why** you want to develop and/or leverage your research use mindset, skills and/or relationships. Why is this important to you? What benefits could this bring? What negative outcomes could be avoided?

You can use the space below to note 1–2 reasons why you think it's important to develop or leverage your research use mindset, skills and/or relationships:

....

....

....

STEP B
IDENTIFY YOUR OWN BEHAVIOURS

Drawing on the practices you have read about in this chapter, use the ATACT template below to identify 1–2 behaviours that you feel you can adopt easily that will improve your research use mindset, skillset and/or relationships.

For example:

> *To get their views about the relevance of the research to our context, once a week (**time**), during our subject/domain leadership team meetings (**context**), I (**actor**) am going to share (**action**) a reading with my colleagues (**target**)."*

ATACT	Behaviour 1	Behaviour 2
ACTOR (Who?)		
TARGET (To what/whom?)		
ACTION (Does what?)		
CONTEXT (Where?)		
TIME (When?)		

Using the space below, you might like to write these as behavioural statements:

....

....

....

....

To support you in making these changes, you might also want to consider and respond to the following:

- Who are you going to consult to check the feasibility of these behaviours?
- What steps are you going to take next to put these changes into action?
- When do you plan to make these changes?

IMPROVEMENT ACTIVITY PART 2
IDENTIFY WHO YOU COULD CONNECT WITH TO IMPROVE YOUR RESEARCH USE CAPABILITIES

Part 2 of this improvement activity will help you to improve your research use capacities through identifying colleagues or experts, within and beyond your school or organisation, who you could connect with to improve your research use.

STEP A
IDENTIFY WHO YOU COULD CONNECT WITH AND WHY

Use the templates below to brainstorm the various colleagues or experts you could connect with to improve your research use knowledge and skills. Try to think not just of people you currently know or connect with but also new people within or beyond your organisation with whom you would like to start a relationship.

Also consider what you could ask them or talk with them about to improve your research use knowledge and skills. It could be helpful to think about the 'Action' in ATACT, so that you can reach out to people with a clear and actionable request.

Colleagues or experts within the school	What you could ask them or talk with them about to improve your knowledge and skills

Colleagues or experts beyond the school	What you could ask them or talk with them about to improve your knowledge and skills

Anyone else?	What you could ask them or talk with them about to improve your knowledge and skills

STEP B
PRIORITISE WHO YOU WOULD LIKE TO CONNECT WITH

Typically, we don't have the time or resources available to contact everyone or action everything we'd like to immediately. This is an opportunity for you to reflect on your list of potential connections (Step A), consider which are of greatest priority for improving your research use knowledge and skills.

Looking through your list of contacts, and considering what you could ask them to improve your knowledge and skills, use the space below to identify 1–3 contacts who you would like to speak to in the next month:

Contact 1: ....

Contact 2: ....

Contact 3: ....

IMPROVEMENT ACTIVITY PART 3
IDENTIFY OPPORTUNITIES WITHIN YOUR SCHOOL OR ORGANISATION TO DEMONSTRATE HOW TO USE RESEARCH WELL

In this chapter, we explored three key elements of demonstrating quality research use, namely:

1. showing others how to use research well;
2. leading a knowledge sharing culture; and
3. promoting the professional value of research use.

Where are the opportunities for you to demonstrate research use in your school or organisation? For example, during regular leadership team meetings, whole-of-school professional development days, inquiry cycle processes or professional learning community sessions. You might like to note these here.

....
....
....
....

How could you demonstrate or model research use actions during these opportunities? For example, you might like to select a new research reading, synthesise this and share your findings, or demonstrate a research-informed practice through a role-play.

....
....
....
....
....

⊙ CHAPTER REVIEW

After reading this chapter:

☐ Are you able to describe the two key practices of modelling quality research use?

☐ Can you identify aspects of Naomi's case study that are actionable within your context?

☐ Have you applied your learning to Parts 1, 2 and 3 of the improvement activity?

☐ Have you engaged in further activities and reading in Appendix 6 to improve how you model quality research use?

NOTE

1. The QURE Assessment Tool is an online self-assessment tool that can be completed by individuals or groups to determine and develop quality research use knowledge and capacities. The tool provides an instantaneous scoring profile and access to tailored scaffolds.

CHAPTER 7
SUPPORTING QUALITY RESEARCH USE

USING RESEARCH WELL INVOLVES YOU:
- providing support for, and fostering a culture supportive of, research use.

SUPPORTING QUALITY RESEARCH USE IS IMPORTANT BECAUSE:
- without support, people are less likely to engage with research in their everyday practice.

PROVIDING SUPPORT HELPS TO AVOID:
- inconsistent or isolated examples of research use across your school or organisation; and
- research use not being seen as an ongoing organisational priority.

THIS CHAPTER WILL HELP YOU TO:
- provide tangible support for research use; and
- build a supportive culture for research use.

LEARN MORE ABOUT SUPPORTING QUALITY RESEARCH USE BY:
- reading about its two key practices;
- engaging with Imogen's case study example;
- completing the improvement activity; and
- exploring Appendix 7 for further activities and reading.

DOI: 10.4324/9781003375845-7   This chapter has been made available under a CC-BY-NC-ND 4.0 license.

INTRODUCTION

> *[Using research well means that] teachers engage in ongoing professional learning, coaching and mentoring and are provided with in-class support and observations. They utilise data [and research] to drive their teaching and are given opportunities to reflect on their practice in a supported and collaborative environment."* **(Senior leader, survey)**

In the previous chapter, we talked about the leadership practice of modelling quality research use and how leaders of all kinds can help others to use research well through 'leading by doing'. This chapter turns now to the leadership practice of supporting quality research use or 'leading by supporting'. It will be helpful if you:

- feel that research use in your context needs to be better supported in some way;
- want to embed research use within your organisational structures and processes; or
- want to build a stronger research use culture within your school or organisation.

There are two aspects of research use support that are important to consider. Firstly, it is critical that **tangible supports for research use** exist in your school or organisation, such as scheduled time and/or relevant professional learning. Secondly, it is important that your organisation has a **culture that supports research use** – for example, individuals feel encouraged to use research in their practice, and there is an ethos of continuous learning and shared responsibility for improving research use. This chapter explores these aspects of supporting quality research use through two key practices:

1. providing tangible support for research use; and
2. building a supportive organisational culture for research use.

These practices are important because for organisations to use research well, individuals within those organisations need to use research to inform their work – yet cannot do so without organisational and system supports. A research-engaged culture that supports and is supportive, therefore, needs to be established by leaders. These practices also help to sustain quality research use over time, reinforcing to people that using research is an organisational priority that requires ongoing support to be done well.

As you read this chapter, you might like to think about how research is used within your school or organisation and consider the following:

- Why is supporting quality research use important to us?
- How could we improve the ways in which we provide research use supports to individuals and groups?
- How supportive is our current culture for research use?
- What changes could we make to our leadership practices to better support others' research use?

◉ KEY PRACTICE 1
PROVIDING TANGIBLE SUPPORT FOR RESEARCH USE

When educators in our work spoke about using research, they often emphasised that it was highly skilled work (referenced in 89% of interviews, 91% of surveys) that required various supports to do well (referenced in 81% of interviews). The types of tangible support that educators valued were both material (e.g., access to research, scheduled time to engage with research), as well as developmental (e.g., access to research use coaches and mentors, specialised professional learning) (see Key Concepts box in Appendix 7). This first key practice of providing support, then, involves:

- embedding research use in meetings;
- building a research resource hub; and
- utilising organisational structures and processes.

EMBEDDING RESEARCH USE IN MEETINGS

In our work, educators stressed the importance of 'build[ing] time into staff schedules for reading, discussing and understanding research' (72% rated as 'important' or 'very important' in third survey). But scheduling such time can be difficult, and as a leader, you may not know where to start, or may feel as if you and your colleagues actually don't have the time to use research at all. Leveraging existing meetings can be a good first step towards building a research-engaged culture.

In your school or organisation, there are likely a **range of existing meetings that are suitable to introduce the use of research**, with some suggestions shown in Table 7.1.

Table 7.1.
Examples of meetings where research use can be discussed and implemented

Whole-of-staff, year level or faculty/subject domain meetings	Regular team or leadership meetings	School review or organisational strategic planning meetings
Professional development meetings, including staff presentation sessions	Individual performance review and planning meetings	Curriculum design/planning meetings

These types of settings are familiar to people and can provide them with opportunities to engage with research in understated and non-threatening ways. They also signal that research use and capacity development are important. As one middle leader emphasised: "If it's structured into what we're doing [in meetings or professional learning], then it makes it easier to find the time to do the reading".

Embedding research use into existing meetings can also enable people to have more regular interactions with research. For example, one senior leader spoke about how research was introduced during regular staff meetings:

> At all of our brief staff meetings that we have at the beginning of each week, the teacher development team usually do a mini presentation. And they always mention research. So, … teachers hear it all the time … making that link all the time between research-and-practice, research-and-practice."

In order for existing meetings to be utilised for research use, though, it is often important to **reprioritise the focus of meetings and think carefully about staff workloads**. These approaches were illustrated by two senior leaders in a primary school who spoke about "want[ing meetings] to be more about research and more about best practice and collaborative planning". They described feeling frustrated that "some meetings were starting to turn into a large amount of admin[istration] and talk" and undertook three key actions to "reduce" this. These actions included:

- reducing weekly 30-minute staff meetings to fortnightly, with changed agendas that focused on "curriculum and pedagogy primarily [and] not managerial [work]";
- establishing communication protocols whereby administrative tasks were communicated and resolved primarily via email, and "then [not] rehash[ed] in a meeting"; and
- shifting the responsibility for certain tasks from teachers to other staff in the school, including reassigning to the principal's executive assistant the entering of students' assessment data into relevant databases.

By taking these actions, the leadership team "built time within school hours to release collaborative groups for either professional learning or research engagement". They went on to explain the benefit of these types of meetings as effective developmental forums:

> So, building that time in and making it valuable … and focused on research and evidence-informed practice. It's short and sweet, but enough. So, it's not arduous, but it keeps [everyone] engaging in research continuously."

BUILDING A RESEARCH RESOURCE HUB

A research resource hub is a physical and/or virtual "place" in your school or organisation where relevant research-related materials are housed (Senior leader, interview). This place might be any combination of a physical library or resource centre, physical or online communal reading and discussion 'spaces', and online platforms or repositories. The range of materials housed in such hubs can be varied, as illustrated by the examples in Table 7.2.

Table 7.2.
Examples of research-related resources

Academic journals and books, including links to relevant databases and online libraries	Research-informed videos and podcasts	Curated research summaries, such as one-page overviews	Research use 'how-to' guides and tools, including links to relevant jurisdiction frameworks and guides
Internal and external professional learning presentations and conference summaries	Induction, professional learning community and/or inquiry cycle materials	Newsletters, articles and research summaries from professional associations or literature	Research-informed lesson plan examples and practice guides

In our work, educators often emphasised **the benefits of building resource hubs**. Firstly, they allow for easy access to research-related materials and information. For example, one senior leader commented during an interview that their "portal" would have "material where it's centralised and can be retrieved at any time", allowing people to read about different research-informed approaches and "[take] into consideration what we think is best practice". Secondly, it encourages individuals to "dig deeper" into research (Senior leader, interview), helping them to formulate different research-informed practice ideas. Finally, such a hub, particularly if there is an associated physical space like a professional reading room, can foster collaborative discussions about research. This was explained by another senior leader from a secondary school during an interview:

> *We've got staff that are just coming here [to our professional reading room] and borrowing stuff, whether they're doing their Masters [post-graduate study] or not. It's been really great for those studying, but also really great for the everyday staff members too, who are just interested in a particular idea as well. So … [it's contributing to] that cultural shift and build as well.*

UTILISING ORGANISATIONAL STRUCTURES AND PROCESSES

There is a range of developmental opportunities that you can provide to help individuals and groups improve their research use. For example, Chapter 6 outlined some internal activities (e.g., reading and reflecting on research use case studies; engaging with the QURE Assessment Tool [bit.ly/quretool] and setting some improvement goals) and external experiences (e.g., participating in research use professional learning courses or attending conferences) that may be suitable for anyone in your school or organisation to undertake. You can also provide research use support by utilising existing or building certain structures and processes within your school or organisation, such as inquiry cycle processes, professional learning communities, and coaching/mentoring structures.

In our work, many educators spoke of **utilising inquiry cycles or short, structured processes repeated over time** as a useful way of combining professional learning, research use capacity building, and practice improvement. These types of processes were often accompanied by professional learning community structures. For example, during interviews, one middle leader described how he had established a formal professional learning cycle that helped his colleagues to unpack and trial a new research-informed teaching approach:

> [Professional learning meetings are] based on a joint book study and we discuss strategies that are recommended in the book. And teachers then, based on those meetings, develop SMART [i.e., specific, measurable, achievable, realistic and time-bound] goals. They work, then, for a fortnightly cycle on those SMART goals. We go into the classrooms and provide teachers with feedback on their practice. And then after a cycle of two weeks, we have another professional learning session where teachers report on the impact of their SMART goal ... how effective it has been, how they've measured the effectiveness. And then we go from there further into the book and [repeat] the same cycle."

Another possible strategy is to **create positions with responsibility for supporting others to develop their research use skills and knowledge** through coaching or mentoring. These roles might be dedicated research leads or heads of resource hubs, learning/instructional leaders, or assistant principals. When educators in our work spoke about coaching/mentoring, they often described role-modelling practices (Chapter 6). For example, during interviews, one school principal described "train[ing] my line managers to be coaches with their line management team". As a part of supporting others, she explained that each leader negotiated a practice improvement focus for each of their teachers, which was then incorporated as a goal in their performance development plans. Coaches role-modelled the new research-informed teaching approaches, and then observed teachers trialling the approaches themselves. She emphasised that "when you put attention on something, you will always improve", and explained that the cascaded coaching program was key to individual teachers' practice improvement:

> *And it's one of those observations where [the coach] just writes everything that happens. So, then they have another meeting, and the coach gets from the teacher what could have been done differently, what worked really well, [etc.]. And then students are [re-]surveyed. And then [teachers] get a graph back which ... will show the degree of improvement. But also, it will show us as a whole school - I get a picture of the efficacy around the teaching that's happening in the school."*

RECAP: PROVIDING TANGIBLE SUPPORT FOR RESEARCH USE

This section has outlined three ways that you can support others in your school or organisation to use research well.

Providing tangible support for research use by:

embedding research use in meetings

building a research resource hub

utilising organisational structures and processes

◈ KEY PRACTICE 2
BUILDING A SUPPORTIVE ORGANISATIONAL CULTURE FOR RESEARCH USE

When educators in our work spoke about using research well, they often emphasised the importance of a supportive organisational culture (referenced in 96% of interviews). One senior leader explained that such a culture "means that [research use] is intrinsic in your language, it's intrinsic in your approach", and requires ongoing and consistent leadership encouragement and support to people. This second key practice of building a research-engaged culture involves:

- encouraging experimentation with research use;
- involving others in leading quality research use; and
- celebrating research use successes.

ENCOURAGING EXPERIMENTATION WITH RESEARCH USE

Providing opportunities for people to "try out" (Senior leader, interview) research-informed approaches is an important feature of a supportive organisational culture. These opportunities might be larger in scale and more formal in nature, such as trialling of a new school-wide research-informed teaching practice (Chapter 5), or smaller in scale and more informal, such as experimenting with a particular approach in one classroom that you had read about in your own time. Encouraging any research use experimentation, though, necessarily involves allowing time and space for things to sometimes fail. In our work, educators spoke of the importance of leadership practices that fostered a "safe" organisational culture (Senior leader, interview), "where informed risk taking [was] encouraged and reflected upon to inform decision making" (Teacher, survey) or where there was "risk taking [and it was] okay to try and fail" (Teacher, survey).

These ideas were captured by one senior leader during an interview when she was describing her school's implementation of a new approach to students' writing:

> *I think it's important to understand that, sometimes, you are experimenting a little bit in these spaces, and sometimes it works really well and other times less so. And then you just [have to] pivot and adjust and try again. We had a really supportive team [and] that really was pretty vital to it."*

In the same interview, an early-career teacher working in the team that was trialling this approach spoke of the supportive leadership attitudes and practices:

> *When you are experimenting with something, I think you want that reassurance - you don't want to try something [and] fail. So, I think particularly what also worked when we were implementing research[ed] strategies was that collaboration. So, having that option to say [to my leader], 'I'm trying this, can you come watch?' Or 'What do you think of this?' And then showing it and getting that second opinion. And I think it relieves you of a lot of not only the accountability but, I guess, the fear of trying it out or being on the wrong track."*

When **encouraging others to experiment with research use**, it is important that leaders are supportive of them making multiple attempts or repeating trials of research-informed approaches. Perseverance is needed by everyone to bring about sustained practice improvement from research use. For example, one senior leader described how leaders in his school encouraged teachers to "keep trying" and supported them by observing, debriefing and amending practice trials. This "trial and error and experimenting" approach eventually led to positive behavioural change, as he went on to explain:

> *There's been a few teachers who have trialled [research-informed approaches], just as a bit of an experiment ... and [with support] have made a concerted effort to change their behaviour through that particular technique."*

INVOLVING OTHERS IN LEADING QUALITY RESEARCH USE

Another feature of a supportive organisational culture is shared responsibility for leading research use. In our work, a number of educators described leveraging or creating distributed leadership models to share responsibilities for building the research use capacities of staff (Chapter 6). Through these types of structures, varied research use-related professional learning experiences can be provided while also building the research use leadership skills of middle leaders.

Distributed leadership for research use can also help to get buy-in from staff to a research-informed change initiative, or it can help to 'spread the message' that research use is a priority. Both of these ideas were reflected in a senior leader's description of how she engaged middle leaders and teachers in the implementation phase of her school's assessment framework redesign initiative:

> *So, for each learning area, we felt [utilising] a team of three or four teachers that were the next level down from the leading teacher [would benefit implementation], just to build that capacity. Because I was really mindful of [the fact that] I'm an assistant principal, and me coming up with a framework and going, 'This is the framework, you all must do this' - that wasn't going to work. My focus was getting my leading teachers onboard and then getting that next level of leadership, the ones who are going to be the early adopters, the ones who are going to get up and actually work this in a classroom, and the ones who were going to be excited by the theory and the idea they'd actually get it running practically."*

Trust can also be built within your organisational culture, which, in turn, can foster increased and improved research use across your school or organisation. One senior leader at a different school described how trust was built through devolving leadership responsibility as they implemented a particular research-informed curriculum initiative:

> *It seemed to be this snowball or a swell of support for embedding real change. And I found, as a leader, that there was significant trust being generated. [For example] I talked to the learning leaders about the evidence [underpinning the initiative's design] and, before you know it, the learning leaders, without me, are really driving it ... And we've had really robust discussions ... I've been*

challenged from the learning leaders. So, it's this culture of mutual trust and we made some changes based on staff challenging some decisions that [were] made ... [there has been] healthy respect and the healthy advice has been very much appreciated."

CELEBRATING RESEARCH USE SUCCESSES

Finally, a supportive research use culture is one where **examples of research use successes are celebrated and promoted**. When people can see positive examples of improvement due to research-informed approaches, several benefits arise. Firstly, they can foster more widespread experimentation with research use, which, in turn, can contribute to professional capacity building across your school or organisation. In our work, for example, one senior leader described celebrating the "pretty good achievement" that all staff within her school had engaged in research use through a "reading circle" initiative that had been implemented as a professional learning structure. She described being proud of the fact "that every teacher in [her] school had done some professional reading this year", which had helped everyone to be more open and confident to engage in new practice ideas.

Secondly, new ideas can lead to improvements in practice and outcomes, which then help to build an organisation-wide commitment to research use over time. This was emphasised by one school principal when he reiterated the importance of celebrating "small wins" from the ongoing implementation of research in his school:

> *Any movement in the data that came from [staff's research use] effort, you've got to celebrate it. Your data can go back at the start ... [sometimes you] can't see the shift at the beginning. So, you've got to stay the course. You've got to be committed, be true to yourself and believe in what you're doing. ... And don't jump off that course, don't go to some other idea. Stick to that research evidence and do it well and persevere with it ... [and then] any incremental shift or change in the data, I'd celebrate it."*

Finally, as described by another senior leader from a different school, when positive outcomes from research use are experienced and made visible, there is potential for an organisational research use culture to be sustained:

> *[Teachers] saw success quickly from engaging in research, which meant the research actually sold itself in the end. From there, that culture of continual improvement and professional learning, but in small bite-size amounts, meant that we could change the culture of the school."*

RECAP: BUILDING A SUPPORTIVE ORGANISATIONAL CULTURE FOR RESEARCH USE

This section has outlined three ways that you can build an organisational culture that is supportive of quality use of research.

Building a supportive research use organisational culture by:

encouraging experimentation with research use

involving others in leading quality research use

celebrating research use successes

CASE STUDY 7.1
WHAT DOES SUPPORTING QUALITY RESEARCH USE LOOK LIKE IN ACTION?

To help you to see how the two key practices discussed in this chapter can work together in action, the following case study illustrates how a primary school leadership team set about providing support for, and fostering a culture supportive of, research use.

Imogen is a principal in a regional government primary school of average socio-economic status. Along with Brooklyn, the Assistant Principal of Curriculum and Instruction, and Sia, a middle school leader, she described how her leadership team had been "very strategic" over recent years to assist "teachers at the grassroots" to use research well in their practice.

PROVIDING TANGIBLE SUPPORT FOR RESEARCH USE

The school provides a combination of material and developmental supports to help people improve their research use. The first of these is focused on providing teachers with scheduled time to engage with research. Over and above the state-legislated two hours of release time away from face-to-face teaching per teacher/per week, Imogen "buys additional time" by recruiting casual staff so that the timetable can be organised to give teaching teams an extra 80 minutes of collaborative time per week. When asked whether any tasks have stopped or been reassigned to "create" this time, Sia explains:

> We don't teach music in the classroom, that's done by the dedicated music teacher. We don't take [the students] to library, that's done by a dedicated library teacher. And that's our 80 minutes – 40 [minutes] for music, 40 [minutes] for library."

Imogen went on to explain that for scheduled time to be "effective", it needs to be directed and measured by leaders. She emphasised that time given "will always be used", but for the time to be productive, it needs to be evaluated in light of individual development goal achievement or improved student learning outcomes.

Upskilling the leadership team in how to use research well is a key priority at the school. Brooklyn fulfils a dedicated research lead role and, along with another assistant principal, takes charge of building the research use capacities of the leaders through weekly structured professional learning sessions, one-on-one coaching, as well as observation and collaborative feedback processes. The aim is for leaders to utilise existing inquiry cycle processes within the school to guide their own teaching staff to use research and implement practice improvements. Brooklyn and her colleague make sure to spend time with leaders and their teams during these cycles to observe how effective sessions are and how well the leaders themselves are coaching and mentoring others around research-informed approaches. These observations then drive both individual tailored coaching for leaders and collective professional learning sessions.

A final tangible support is a "practice hub" - an online platform managed by Brooklyn and that houses research, advice and guidelines, professional learning examples, practice approaches and case studies, amongst other helpful information.

BUILDING A SUPPORTIVE ORGANISATIONAL CULTURE FOR RESEARCH USE

From the outset, Imogen was passionate about establishing a supportive research use culture in the school:

> *It's about supporting teachers to be the best that they can be through using research and engaging in that research to make change and practice improvement in the classroom to impact the learning outcomes of their kids."*

While she has a "vision" for and "commitment" to quality research use herself, she believes that a particular "leadership mindset" is critical in helping to shape the school culture. She is conscious that she needs to bring her leaders along on the journey: "We're not there yet, but we've come a long way. We've still got a lot to do to embed the effective use of research". Providing support and being supportive to leaders is therefore critical:

> *In reality, different people have a different understanding of the importance of research. ... So we are supporting all of our leaders to get a common understanding of its importance and how it underpins different strategies. ... We're not about telling someone what to do, but we are about helping them understand the 'why' of what we do. And that's why we use research – to understand the 'why' of what we do and the impact of that."*

Supporting leaders to ask questions in a safe and trusting environment and allowing them time to experiment with research are key principles that underpin the school's research use culture. As a part of monthly structured staff professional learning meetings, Brooklyn leads group reflection sessions that help people to feel supported in their use of research and celebrate learnings, as well as help leaders to gain valuable insights into what constitutes a supportive organisational culture. Imogen believes that these reflection sessions are critical for evaluating the effectiveness of different research use supports provided. Acting on this knowledge is key, as she observes:

> *If you don't actually act on it, you're not learning anything from it. And so that's why each year [our support of research use] has changed. Not a heap, but a little bit. ... Because the moment you change it [a lot], that's when you don't get everyone on board."*

Finally, "staying the course" and acknowledging what's working well help Imogen and her leaders to build a supportive culture for research use over time. As she explains:

> *It is about consistency. [It is not about] 'What do we need to do next?', [it is about] 'How does it need to evolve?' ... We're at the point where our current strategy is the best that it can be – we just need to put that into practice for longer and then we will get there."*

◑ PUTTING THINGS INTO PRACTICE
HOW CAN I SUPPORT QUALITY RESEARCH USE?

This final section is designed to help you to move from understanding how to support quality research use to enacting it within your context. The section features an improvement activity that will help you and your colleagues to identify research use practices you would like to support, and explore what you could do to champion them within your team, school or organisation.

The activity is designed in two parts:

- **Part 1** builds on your knowledge of behaviours (from Chapters 2 and 6) and helps you to identify research use actions that you would like to support in your context.
- **Part 2** guides you through a behaviour change tool to explore different ways you could support the identified research use practices from Part 1.

You can choose to complete these activity parts individually and/or with colleagues as a team.

We also encourage you to:

Look at Appendix 7 where you might like to:

- Use the practice checklist to determine how well you believe that you are currently applying the key practices outlined in this chapter and respond to the reflection prompts.
- Engage with Seadale Primary School's case study, which features examples of ways to support quality research use.
- Lead a *Q Conversation* about strengthening your school or organisation evidence use culture.
- Learn more about the key concepts used in this chapter.
- Use the QURE Assessment Tool (bit.ly/quretool) with a group of colleagues to assess your school's or organisation's use of research and access tailored scaffolds that will support your improvement.
- Read more about behavioural change and the EAST Framework (Service et al., 2014), which features in Part 2 of the Improvement Activity.

Initiate a group conversation in your school or organisation about supporting quality research use. This conversation might involve you comparing and discussing your responses to the improvement activity and/or your practice checklist ratings in Appendix 7. Or, as a group, you might like to discuss the reflective questions that were posed in the introduction section of this chapter.

IMPROVEMENT ACTIVITY PART 1
IDENTIFY QUALITY RESEARCH USE ACTIONS YOU WOULD LIKE TO SUPPORT

This chapter discusses the importance of supporting others in your school or organisation to use research well – in particular, encouraging research use by providing tangible support and by building a supportive research use culture.

Part 1 of this improvement activity will help you to identify quality research use actions that you would like to support in your school or organisation.

The improvement activity in Chapter 2 introduced you to behaviours and the ATACT framework, and Chapter 6 built on this knowledge. If you would like to practise identifying and articulating behaviours before applying the ATACT framework in this chapter, please revisit Chapter 2. You can also review the key behaviours performed by Imogen and Brooklyn to support research use in their school (see case study in this chapter), which we have highlighted below.

WHAT BEHAVIOURS WERE PERFORMED BY IMOGEN AND BROOKLYN?

Three key actions were taken by Imogen and Brooklyn to support research use in their school. Using the ATACT framework, these can be articulated as behaviours as follows:

1. Through contracting casual staff, Imogen (**actor**) schedules release time from teaching (**action**) for staff teams (**target**) each week (**time**) while at school (**context**), which enables them to collectively engage with research.
2. Brooklyn (**actor**) provides professional learning sessions (**action**) to school leaders (**target**) each week (**time**) during one-on-one or group meetings (**context**) to help them build their research use capacities.
3. Brooklyn (**actor**) leads reflection sessions (**action**) with staff (**target**) during monthly (**time**) structured professional development meetings (**context**) to help them feel supported in their use of research and celebrate learnings.

STEP A
IDENTIFY RESEARCH USE GAPS IN YOUR CONTEXT

Drawing on the key practices described in this chapter, what are 1–3 quality research use actions you would like to see more of amongst your colleagues or teams within your school or organisation?

Use the space below to describe 1–3 actions.

STEP B
SPECIFY RESEARCH USE BEHAVIOURS TO BE SUPPORTED

Drawing on the actions you have described above, use the ATACT template below to identify 1–2 behaviours that you would like to support within your school or organisation.

For example:

> Teachers (**actor**) create a formal implementation plan (**action**) with at least one school-based research lead (**target**) every time (**time**) they design a new initiative (**context**)."

ATACT	Behaviour 1	Behaviour 2
ACTOR (Who?)		
TARGET (To what/whom?)		
ACTION (Does what?)		
CONTEXT (Where?)		
TIME (When?)		

Using the space below, you might like to write these as behavioural statements:

....

....

....

....

IMPROVEMENT ACTIVITY PART 2
IDENTIFY WAYS THAT YOU COULD SUPPORT QUALITY RESEARCH USE

In Part 1, you identified 1–2 specific research use behaviours you would like to support.

In Part 2, you will identify different ways these behaviours could be supported within your school or organisation. To do this, we will first highlight some common barriers to action and ways to overcome these barriers, drawing on a particular behaviour change tool. We will then guide you through the application of this tool to explore different ways that you could support the research use behaviours you identified in Part 1.

STEP A
UNDERSTANDING STRATEGIES TO OVERCOME COMMON BARRIERS TO ACTION

The EAST framework (Service et al., 2014) is a behavioural change tool based on four key principles – that is, behaviour change is more likely to occur if you make it **Easy**, **Attractive**, **Social** and **Timely**. Each of these principles is outlined in more detail below:

E	Make it **Easy**: People are more likely to do something when it is relatively easy in terms of thinking and capability. This means that reducing the effort required can increase action.
A	Make it **Attractive**: People are more likely to do something when their attention has been captured. This means it could help to make research use practices personal, relevant and meaningful, or to create a sense of urgency, or to emphasise costs and benefits.
S	Make it **Social**: People are influenced by what others do and expect. This means it can help to draw on credible sources and contacts to support the action, and/or to highlight people who are already performing the behaviour.
T	Make it **Timely**: People are less likely to act when the request comes at the wrong time. This means we should try to prompt action when people are more available and receptive.

Can you identify which EAST principle could be used to address common barriers to action?

For each set of barriers below (1–4), identify which principle aims to address it (E-A-S-T).

	Common barriers to action, applied to research use	Which EAST principle could be used to address this?
1	The research or the research use is unappealing, doesn't feel useful or meaningful. Staff are unlikely to do the action because: "*That's not relevant to me*" or "*I can't see a clear benefit*".	
2	The research or research use is required at a time when the person is unavailable or distracted by other priorities. Staff are unlikely to do the action because: "*I missed the opportunity*" or "*I can't do it right now*".	
3	The research or the research use requires several steps, is complicated or time-consuming. Staff might not do the action because: "*It's a big ask*" or "*It's too much hassle*".	
4	The research or research use isn't visible or promoted by others. Staff might not do the action because: "*Nobody else does*" or "*Close members of my team discourage or don't care about it*".	

STEP B
APPLY EAST TO THE RESEARCH USE BEHAVIOURS YOU WANT TO SUPPORT

The research use behaviours identified in Part 1 were:

Behaviour 1

Behaviour 2

Use the guiding questions below to explore possible ways you could support each of the research use behaviours you identified in Part 1.

Tip: At this stage, don't worry about finding the 'right' or 'best' way – instead, we encourage you to note any and all ideas that come to mind! Later, you can distil your list of potential strategies.

EAST Principle	Applied to Behaviour 1	Applied to Behaviour 2
How can I/we make it Easy?		
• How could the 'hassle' factor be reduced? Where can effort or friction be reduced?		
• How can messages or information be simplified?		
• How can any required actions be broken down into simpler, easier elements?		
How can I/we make it Attractive?		
• How can actions be made more personally relevant?		
• How can I/we draw people's attention?		
• Can incentives or rewards be provided?		
How can I/we make it Social?		
• How can actions be linked to others or require a social commitment?		
• How can I/we promote the actions that are being taken?		
• Can required actions be encouraged or supported through established networks and groups in the school/organisation?		
How can I/we make it Timely?		
• When are staff likely to be most (or more) able to do the action?		
• When are staff most (or more) receptive to what actions are being promoted? When are good times to prompt action?		
• Are there opportunities to leverage times for action when there is already a captive audience?		

STEP C
DISTIL YOUR LIST OF PRIORITY STRATEGIES

Review the list of strategies that have emerged from your work in Step B above and, using the template below, note 1–3 strategies that stand out immediately for you as a priority. You might like to consider certain prioritisation criteria, such as effectiveness of the strategy or potential impact, acceptability of the strategy by staff, and feasibility of implementation.

After noting these strategies, you might want to refine the list further or move to implementing some or all of them. Chapter 5 focuses on implementing research thoughtfully and will be a useful next step for you (if you have not already engaged with this chapter) to refine and/or implement these strategies.

Proposed strategy	This stands out as a priority strategy because:
1.	
2.	
3.	

○ CHAPTER REVIEW

After reading this chapter:

☐ Are you able to describe the two key practices of supporting quality research use?

☐ Can you identify aspects of Imogen's case study that are actionable within your context?

☐ Have you applied your learning to Parts 1 and 2 of the improvement activity?

☐ Have you engaged in further activities and reading in Appendix 7 to improve your knowledge and skills regarding supporting using research well?

CHAPTER 8
CONCLUSION – CONTINUING THE JOURNEY

USING RESEARCH WELL INVOLVES YOU:
- embracing it as a journey, remembering the importance of learning and valuing the development of your expertise.

EMBRACING USING RESEARCH WELL AS A JOURNEY IS IMPORTANT BECAUSE:
- it is skilled work that takes time to develop for individuals, organisations, and systems; and
- it is an area of education that practitioners, policy makers, and researchers are only just starting to explore.

EMBRACING USING RESEARCH WELL AS A JOURNEY HELPS TO AVOID:
- research-informed practice being either a short-lived 'one and done'-type initiative or an unchanging 'set and forget'-type initiative; and
- research-informed development being either 'imposed' on schools or 'patchy' within systems.

THIS CHAPTER WILL HELP YOU TO:
- consider how to sustain your journey with using research well in terms of steps that you can take in your context.

LEARN MORE ABOUT CONTINUING YOUR JOURNEY WITH USING RESEARCH WELL BY:
- engaging with the chapter's main sections and examples.

DOI: 10.4324/9781003375845-8 This chapter has been made available under a CC-BY-NC-ND 4.0 license.

INTRODUCTION

In this book, we have covered a lot of ground from first introducing the idea of quality use of research or using research well (Chapter 1) to then diving into the processes of identifying a specific issue (Chapter 2), finding relevant research (Chapter 3), thoughtfully engaging with (Chapter 4) and implementing (Chapter 5) that research, and then understanding how to model (Chapter 6) and support (Chapter 7) using research well as a practice.

In this final chapter, we look to the future in terms of how you might continue your journey with using research well. We highlight three key ideas connected to:

- journey – embracing your journey with using research well;
- learning – remembering the importance of your learning; and
- expertise – valuing the development of your expertise.

These ideas are important because there is always a risk that, within the busyness of schools and school systems, the practice and value of using research well can get lost. As a result, these three ideas are invitations to consider how the development of quality use of research can be actively sustained over time.

○ JOURNEY – EMBRACING YOUR JOURNEY WITH USING RESEARCH WELL

In Chapter 1, we talked about using research well as a 'developmental practice' that takes time to evolve. Like the development of any skill or practice, getting better at it is an ongoing process (or journey) for individuals, organisations, and systems. Acknowledging your distinctive starting points and allowing time for your research use capacities and practices to develop is therefore one way to embrace using research well as a journey. Also important is remembering that using research well involves lots of different processes (such as identifying a clear purpose, selecting appropriate research, and so on) that themselves take time to develop and interconnect.

Embracing your journey with using research well, then, means:

- allowing time for your research use practices to evolve, research use capacities to develop, and research-informed improvements to materialise;
- being strategic in where you focus your development efforts, including which practice areas, which aspects of research use, and whose research use capacities are prioritised;
- taking a behavioural lens to break your journey down into clear, specific and action-focused steps that can help to engage others in the process;

- holding on to the idea that using research well is about developing your professional and organisational capability that goes beyond any one issue or initiative; and
- being open to refining your research use vision and modifying your research use approach in response to new practice needs, research ideas and impact insights.

WHAT CAN 'EMBRACING YOUR JOURNEY WITH USING RESEARCH WELL' LOOK LIKE IN ACTION?

Starting small

❝ *Starting off small in a particular area is a great idea. ... It's sort of [like] small is the new big, so you're making incremental progress versus trying to change everything at once because that's too overwhelming. ... It's also valuing what's working really well in your school, looking at small areas to improve on and then making tiny changes to practice that are not overwhelming."* (Senior leader, interview)

Staying the course

❝ *You've got to stay the course. You've got to be committed, be true to yourself and believe in what you're doing. You've got to have that belief. So some people give up because they don't see the immediate change. But you've got to believe in it and stay the course. Don't go to some other idea. Stick to that research evidence and do it well and persevere with it."* (Senior leader, interview)

Playing the long game

❝ *Our journey for building a culture of professional learning has taken a long time, but I think that was valuable to take the long time because it means it's been embedded. Like it's just [in] everything that we do [now]."* (Senior leader, interview)

⊙ LEARNING – REMEMBERING THE IMPORTANCE OF YOUR LEARNING

The idea that using research well is a 'sophisticated practice' was introduced early on in Chapter 1. Then, throughout subsequent chapters we have seen the importance of qualities such as thoughtfulness, judiciousness, reflectiveness, and so on. All of these qualities underline the professionalism that is integral to educators and leaders using research well in practice. They remind us that using research well is a process of active professional learning, not passive knowledge transfer. In other words, learning is the fuel that drives the journey of using research well. Another important way to sustain using research well over time, therefore, is to remain mindful about the value of your learning and the need for a culture that prioritises, invests in, and values such learning.

Remembering the importance of your learning means:

- prioritising the continued development of your organisational culture to promote learning, encourage risk-taking, and support reflection;
- creating space, time, and processes within your setting for shared deliberation, discussion, questioning, reflection, consideration, and evaluation of your research use;
- developing and supporting new opportunities for research-related professional learning and capacity building within and beyond your organisation; and
- holding firm to the principle that using research well is highly professional and intricately connected to teaching well and leading well.

WHAT CAN 'REMEMBERING THE IMPORTANCE OF YOUR LEARNING' LOOK LIKE IN ACTION?

Remaining curious

❝ *For me, the most important thing has been to remain curious. … When I started out as a middle leader… I felt I needed to justify my position by seeming immediately competent. Instead, I took it slow, asked lots of questions and connected with my colleagues [in order to gain from] the wealth of knowledge they could offer about using research well."* (Middle leader, interview)

Scheduling time

❝ *Personally, I have put aside time in my calendar each week dedicated to research. For too many, accessing research is seen as a luxury to be had, often done outside of formal working hours. By structuring time in your working week to do research provides one example of how to sustain the practice of engaging with research."* (Senior leader, interview)

Focusing on improvement

❝ *I think curiosity goes to the heart of being a lifelong learner in order to improve my practice as a practitioner, as a leader, in order to find new tools myself [and] evidence-based research that tells me that I can improve my practice and that I can improve student outcomes. So it is a real thirst for improving my own practice to improve student outcomes."* (Middle leader, interview)

⊙ EXPERTISE – VALUING THE DEVELOPMENT OF YOUR EXPERTISE

Early on in this book, we explained how using research well is a 'hidden practice' that has not been discussed very much within the field of education. The knowledge base about using research well in education is therefore still developing. Practitioners like you have a critical contribution to make to growing this knowledge base because it is in contexts of practice that the professionalism of using research well is developed. Remember that all of the practices, examples, and insights that you have read about in this book come from real-life teachers and leaders like you reflecting on what they have learnt about using research well to drive improvement in their school. Valuing your development of this kind of expertise is therefore another important part of your sustaining using research well over time.

Valuing the development of your expertise means:

- noticing and celebrating the growth of your knowledge, skills and capacities related to using research well;
- standing by the idea that using research well is a distinctive aspect of your professional expertise as an educator and a leader;
- looking for opportunities to share and discuss your insights, experiences and lessons with others within and beyond your organisation; and
- remembering that the knowledge base about using research is just developing and needs the expertise of practitioners like you to grow.

WHAT CAN 'VALUING THE DEVELOPMENT OF YOUR EXPERTISE' LOOK LIKE IN ACTION?

Being conscious of your growth

> [I have] become consciously competent around the use of research [and] become consciously competent about leading teachers in the use of research." (Middle leader, interview)

Incorporating research as part of your expertise

> The real power ... is that connection of the research to our own stories, our own data, our own evidence, our own insights about our classrooms and our schools. Bringing research together with the professional judgment and expertise of our teachers and leaders. ... So research doesn't sit out there, it's incorporated. It's really authentically incorporated." (System leader, interview)

Valuing the expertise of other educators

> In addition to trusting quality research, I recommend reaching out to leaders in schools who are using evidence-based practices and can provide an overview of how research can be applied in a school context." (Senior leader, interview)

In conclusion, these three ideas of journey, learning and expertise provide a way to think about how to sustain the development of using research well over time. They remind us that using research well is: a developmental practice that needs to be embraced as a journey; a sophisticated practice that needs to be fuelled by learning; and a hidden practice that needs to be noticed and valued as a particular form of expertise.

All of these considerations are important not just for educators and leaders but also for the education systems in which they work. As a system leader who took part in our work explained: "Thinking about [quality research use] as a general capability is important at the systemic level ... so that systems ... are really thinking about 'How is this capability showing up across our system in how we support schools and in our own work within departments?'".

To this end, we hope that this book helps not only educators and leaders to develop using research well as a capability within their practice, but also system leaders and evidence brokers to support using research well as a culture within schools and systems.

RECAP: CONTINUING THE JOURNEY OF USING RESEARCH WELL

The above sections have highlighted three ways that you can continue your journey with using research well.

Continuing to use research well by:

embracing your journey with using research well

remembering the importance of your learning

valuing the development of your expertise

◎ CHAPTER REVIEW

After reading this chapter:

☐ Are you able to explain why actively sustaining using research well over time is important for schools and systems?

☐ Can you identify how educators and leaders can sustain using research well by embracing it as a journey, remembering the importance of learning, and valuing the development of expertise?

☐ Have you identified some ways in which you can continue your own journey with using research well?

APPENDIX 1
INTRODUCTION - USING RESEARCH WELL

ADDITIONAL CASE STUDY
DEVELOPING RESEARCH USE THROUGH PROFESSIONAL LEARNING

To find out more about improving the use of research within a specific organisation, you can engage with Teresa's case study (bit.ly/teresacasestudy) about developing research use through professional learning.

You might like to respond to the considerations at the end of the case study and/or initiate a group discussion about the case study in your school or organisation.

FURTHER READING
USING RESEARCH WELL

If you are interested in learning more about using research well, you can read the Q Project's:

- report about the *Quality Use of Research Evidence (QURE) Framework* (Rickinson et al., 2020) (15 pages);
- journal article about the development of the *QURE Framework* (Rickinson et al., 2022) (26 pages);
- report about what using research well look like in Australian schools (Rickinson et al., 2021) (40 pages);
- journal article about practitioner perspectives on using research well (Gleeson et al., 2023) (20 pages); and
- book about what it means to use research well in education (Rickinson et al., 2024) (214 pages).

REFERENCES

Coldwell, M., Greany, T., Higgins, S., Brown, C., Maxwell, B., Stiell, B., Stoll, L., Willis, B., & Burns, H. (2017). *Evidence-informed teaching: An evaluation of progress in England: Research report*. Department for Education. https://www.gov.uk/government/publications/evidence-informed-teaching-evaluation-of-progress-in-england

Gleeson, J., Rickinson, M., Walsh, L., Cutler, B., Salisbury, M., Hall, G., & Khong, H. (2023) Quality use of research evidence: Practitioner perspectives. *Evidence & Policy*, *19*(3), 423–443. https://doi.org/10.1332/174426421X16778434724277

Gough, D., Maidment, C., & Sharples, J. (2018). *UK What Works Centres: Aims, methods and contexts*. EPPI-Centre, Social Science Research Unit, UCL Institute of Education, University College London. https://eppi.ioe.ac.uk/cms/Default.aspx?tabid=3731

Nelson, J., Mehta, P., Sharples, J., & Davey, C. (2017). *Measuring teachers' research engagement: Findings from a pilot study*. Education Endowment Foundation. https://educationendowmentfoundation.org.uk/projects-and-evaluation/evaluation/eef-evaluation-reports-and-research-papers/methodological-research-and-innovations/measuring-teachers-research-engagement

Plant, B., Boulet, M., & Smith, L. (2022). *A behavioural approach to understanding and encouraging quality use of research evidence in Australian schools*. BehaviourWorks Australia. https://doi.org/10.26180/21530658.v1

Rickinson, M., Cirkony, C., Walsh, L., Gleeson, J., Cutler, B., & Salisbury, M. (2022). A framework for understanding the quality of evidence use in education. *Educational Research, 64*(2), 133–158. https://doi.org/10.1080/00131881.2022.2054452

Rickinson, M., Gleeson, J., Walsh, L., Salisbury, M., Cutler, B., & Cirkony, C. (2021). *Using research well in Australian schools: Discussion paper*. Monash University. https://doi.org/10.26180/14783637.v2

Rickinson, M., Walsh, L., Cirkony, C., Salisbury, M., & Gleeson, J. (2020). *Quality use of research evidence framework*. Monash University. https://doi.org/10.26180/14071508.v2

Rickinson, M., Walsh, L., Gleeson, J., & Cutler, B. (2023). *The Q Project: Improving the use of research evidence in Australian schools*. Open Science Framework. https://doi.org/10.17605/OSF.IO/V27FX

Rickinson, M., Walsh, L., Gleeson, J., Cutler, B., Cirkony, C., & Salisbury, M. (2024). *Understanding the quality use of research evidence in education: What it means to use research well*. Routledge. https://doi.org/10.4324/9781003353966

APPENDIX 2
IDENTIFYING A CLEAR PURPOSE

ANSWERS
IMPROVEMENT ACTIVITY PART 2

In Part 2 of the Improvement Activity in Chapter 2, you were asked to practise defining purposeful research use behaviours by drawing on Sascha's case study.

Sascha undertook a number of behaviours to explain and/or promote the purpose of research use. Using the ATACT framework, these can be articulated as behaviours as follows:

1. During the whole-of-school presentation day (time) at the school (context), Sascha (actor) presented evidence of issues with their current assessment model (action) to staff (target).
2. To confirm whether the assessment issue was a priority to address, Sascha (actor) conducted a question-answer session (action) with all staff (target) during the whole-of-school presentation day (time) at the school (context).
3. To identify initiatives that could be stopped or reconfigured to align with the strategic design of the new assessment model, Sascha (actor) facilitated a session (action) at the school (context) with learning leaders (target) prior to the whole-of-school presentation day (time).
4. During the whole-of-school presentation day (time) at the school (context), Sascha (actor) explained the decision to stop or reconfigure initiatives to align with the new assessment model (action) to staff (target).

ADDITIONAL ACTIVITY
PRACTICE CHECKLIST

Use the following checklist to determine how well you believe that you are currently applying the key practices outlined in Chapter 2.

You can complete this checklist yourself and use your responses to target 1–2 practices that you might want to improve. Or you might want to consider asking colleagues to read the chapter, complete the checklist and then initiate a group discussion to compare responses and potentially compile a collective improvement action plan.

Specifying an improvement need to drive your research use	Not yet	Yes, but	Doing well	Not applicable now[a]
Mapped evidence types and sources to gather and analyse	☐	☐	☐	☐
Formulated questions to help analyse evidence	☐	☐	☐	☐
Invited colleagues to help gather and analyse evidence	☐	☐	☐	☐
Analysed evidence from different perspectives and over time	☐	☐	☐	☐
Consulted with colleagues to check for bias and consider different contextual perspectives	☐	☐	☐	☐
Determined the criteria and process for selecting a priority need	☐	☐	☐	☐
Selected a priority need that is specific and focused	☐	☐	☐	☐

Promoting and explaining the purpose for using research	Not yet	Yes, but	Doing well	Not applicable now
Communicated to others the purpose of research use and the selection process	☐	☐	☐	☐
Ensured consistent messaging about research use purpose in all communications	☐	☐	☐	☐
Embedded research use purpose within organisational plans and processes	☐	☐	☐	☐
Linked research-informed change to organisational strengths in communication	☐	☐	☐	☐

a. It may be that some of the checklist points are not applicable to your current focus, in which case, tick 'Not applicable now'. However, if they are relevant, we encourage you to record whether they are: not happening yet ('Not yet'), happening but with some challenges ('Yes, but'), or happening well ('Doing well').

ADDITIONAL REFLECTION
PRACTICE CHECKLIST CONSIDERATIONS

Use the space below to reflect on the following considerations. You can do this individually or with others.

- What results were surprising? Where is there room for growth?
- What changes could be made in response?
- Why are these changes important to you?

....

....

....

....

....

ADDITIONAL CASE STUDY
PURPOSEFUL RESEARCH USE

If you would like to read more about what purposeful research use looks like in action, you can engage with Jason's case study (bit.ly/jasoncasestudy) about contextual research use in his secondary school. You might like to respond to the considerations posed at the end of the case study and/or initiate a group discussion about the case study in your school or organisation.

FURTHER INFORMATION
KEY CONCEPTS

In Chapter 2, you were introduced to the practice of analysing a variety of evidence to help you specify a need for improvement in your school or organisation. The following Key Concepts box helps you to understand the differences between evidence types.

> **TYPES OF EVIDENCE**
>
> A helpful way to think about the different kinds of evidence that educators can draw on is in terms of:
>
> - **Data-based evidence** – such as student assessment and attitudinal data and/or school management data;
> - **Practice-based evidence** – such as teacher assessments, professional judgements and/or professional enquiries; and
> - **Research-based evidence** – such as peer-reviewed systematic reviews, research studies and/or evaluations.
>
> Each of these evidence types can inform educational improvement in different ways but are most powerful when used in combination.
>
> Source: Nelson and Campbell (2019)

FURTHER READING
QUALITY USE OF RESEARCH EVIDENCE (QURE) BEHAVIOURS

In the improvement activity in Chapter 2, you were introduced to the concept of behaviours and asked to define some changes that you could make to improve your purposeful use of research.

If you are interested in learning more about key behaviours that underpin the quality use of research and how these behaviours can be facilitated at individual (educator), organisational, and education system levels, you can read BehaviourWorks Australia's report about *A Behavioural Approach to Understanding and Encouraging Quality Use of Research Evidence* (Plant et al., 2022) (48 pages).

REFERENCES

Nelson, J., & Campbell, C. (2019). Using evidence in education. In A. Boaz, A. Frances & S. M. Nutley (Eds.), *What works now? Evidence-informed policy and practice* (pp. 131–145). Policy Press.

Plant, B., Boulet, M., & Smith, L. (2022). *A behavioural approach to understanding and encouraging quality use of research evidence in Australian schools.* BehaviourWorks Australia. https://doi.org/10.26180/21530658.v1

Presseau, J., McCleary, N., Lorencatto, F., Patey, A. M., Grimshaw, J. M., & Francis, J. J. (2019). Action, actor, context, target, time (AACTT): A framework for specifying behaviour. *Implementation Science, 14*(1), 1–13. https://doi.org/10.1186/s13012-019-0951-x

APPENDIX 3
SELECTING APPROPRIATE RESEARCH

ADDITIONAL ACTIVITY
PRACTICE CHECKLIST

Use the following checklist to review how well you are currently applying the key practices discussed in Chapter 3.

You can complete this checklist yourself and use your responses to target one to two practices that you might want to improve. Or you might want to consider asking colleagues to read the chapter, complete the checklist and then initiate a group discussion to compare responses and potentially compile a collective improvement action plan.

Determining which research is trustworthy and relevant	Not yet	Yes, but	Doing well	Not applicable now[a]
Determined how you want to use research	☐	☐	☐	☐
Explored how different types of research and their insights are suitable	☐	☐	☐	☐
Earmarked the types of research that will be most appropriate	☐	☐	☐	☐
Identified important factors in your context	☐	☐	☐	☐
Considered what 'fit' you will seek between research and your context	☐	☐	☐	☐
Discussed what colleagues are looking for in trustworthy and useful research	☐	☐	☐	☐
Identified what 'markers' you will look for in trustworthy research	☐	☐	☐	☐
Explored research formats that may be useful	☐	☐	☐	☐

(Continued)

Searching for research widely and strategically	Not yet	Yes, but	Doing well	Not applicable now
Selected sources of research that align with your needs	☐	☐	☐	☐
Leveraged professional networks to access research sources	☐	☐	☐	☐
Explored how sources could be used in combination	☐	☐	☐	☐
Developed key words to guide your searches	☐	☐	☐	☐
Investigated the search functions of your chosen sources	☐	☐	☐	☐
Established search strategies for your selected sources (e.g., search strings)	☐	☐	☐	☐
Created a reading strategy to effectively scan your search results	☐	☐	☐	☐
Made initial appraisals of research that might be appropriate	☐	☐	☐	☐
Earmarked promising research to take forward, keeping an open mind about how it may support practice	☐	☐	☐	☐

a. It may be that some of the checklist points are not applicable to your current focus, in which case, tick 'Not applicable now'. However, if they are relevant, we encourage you to record whether they are: not happening yet ('Not yet'), happening but with some challenges ('Yes, but'), or happening well ('Doing well').

ADDITIONAL REFLECTION
PRACTICE CHECKLIST CONSIDERATIONS

Use the space below to reflect on the following considerations. You can do this individually or with others.

- What results were surprising? Where is there room for growth?
- What changes could be made in response?
- Why are these changes important to you?

....

....

....

....

....

....

ADDITIONAL CASE STUDIES
SELECTING APPROPRIATE RESEARCH

If you would like to read more about what selecting appropriate research looks like in action, you can engage with Emmanuel and Jades' case study about understanding different research types and uses in their secondary school (bit.ly/emmanueljadecasestudy) and/ or Genevieve's case study about appraising research in her primary special school (bit.ly/genevievecasestudy).

You might like to respond to the considerations posed at the end of each case study and/or initiate a group discussion about one or both case studies in your school or organisation.

FURTHER INFORMATION
KEY CONCEPTS

In Chapter 3, you were introduced to the idea that different kinds of research can be better suited to different kinds of use. The Key Concepts box below explains some common types of research in education.

RESEARCH TYPES

Different types of research serve different aims, draw different conclusions, and make different claims (Kervin et al., 2016). Some common research types in education are:

- **Descriptive research** aims to investigate, describe, and better understand a concept, phenomenon, or experience (e.g., investigating teachers' views of how research informs their practice). These studies will often be qualitative, making use of interviews, observations, and document analyses. However, they can also be quantitative or mixed methods, or they may also draw on philosophy and theory to think differently about a specific phenomenon.
- **Comparative research** aims to investigate relationships and differences between different variables (e.g., exploring if there's a relationship between strong feelings of belonging and students' academic performance). This type of research is often quantitative, using surveys and student data, but sometimes draws on qualitative and mixed methods approaches. Importantly, though, comparative research does not aim to establish causal relationships.
- **Experimental research** aims to test hypotheses in a specific manner to establish causal relationships (e.g., to measure the impact of a specific intervention on students' numeracy levels). Experimental studies are highly structured quantitative studies, such as randomised control trials.
- **Systematic reviews** aim to synthesise the findings of previous research studies on a specific topic or question in an explicit and transparent way (e.g., synthesising the findings of recent research on the impacts of anti-bullying programmes). Meta-analyses are a specific type of systematic review that involves statistical aggregation of the findings from prior studies. Systematic reviews generally, though, can be based on quantitative and/or qualitative studies.

FURTHER READINGS/ACTIVITIES
EXPLORING SOURCES AND USES OF QUALITY RESEARCH

In Chapter 3, the Key Practices and Improvement Activity emphasised the importance of determining what appropriate research means to you and then searching for that research widely and strategically.

If you are interested in learning more about the sources and uses of research, and different ways of appraising their trustworthiness, you might like to engage with the following resources:

- *Q Data Insight* is a resource designed to provide quick insights into how Australian educators engage with research and prompt reflection about how these might apply to your own work. This *Q Data Insight* focuses on how educators source, appraise and use research and evidence in their practice (bit.ly/qdatasources). This may provide some useful pointers when you are thinking about how you will use research, where you will source it, and what 'markers' of trustworthiness and usefulness you will look for.
- Nutley et al.'s (2013) *What Counts as Good Evidence?* provocation paper (40 pages) provides an insightful and accessible discussion about different ways that the quality of evidence can be assessed and how research can connect with practice. It may help extend your thinking about what constitutes trustworthy research in your work.

REFERENCES

Kervin, L., Vialle, W., Howard, S., Herrington, J., & Okely, T. (2016). *Research for educators* (2nd ed.). Cengage Learning.

Nutley, S. M., Powell, A. E., & Davies, H. T. O. (2013). *What counts as good evidence?* Alliance for Useful Evidence. https://hdl.handle.net/10023/3518

SOURCES DISCUSSED BY EDUCATORS

If you would like more information on the sources mentioned by educators in Chapter 3, refer to the reference list below:

Jensen, E. (2013). *Engaging students with poverty in mind: Practical strategies for raising achievement.* Association for Supervision and Curriculum Development (ASCD).

APPENDIX 4
ENGAGING WITH RESEARCH THOUGHTFULLY

ADDITIONAL ACTIVITY
PRACTICE CHECKLIST

Use the following checklist to rate how well you are currently applying the key practices discussed in Chapter 4.

You can complete this checklist yourself and use your responses to target one or two practices that you might want to improve. Or you might want to consider asking colleagues to read the chapter, complete the checklist, and then initiate a group discussion to compare responses and potentially compile a collective improvement action plan.

Interpreting research and understanding its possible implications	Not yet	Yes, but	Doing well	Not applicable now[a]
Asked critical questions of the research you have selected	☐	☐	☐	☐
Explored how research insights fit with other evidence and your expertise	☐	☐	☐	☐
Taken time to develop a deep understanding of the research	☐	☐	☐	☐
Worked collaboratively to develop your understanding of the research	☐	☐	☐	☐
Been open-minded and reflective about how the research might inform your work	☐	☐	☐	☐
Clarified the implications of the research for your specific improvement need	☐	☐	☐	☐
Discerned what research insights you will take forward into practice	☐	☐	☐	☐
Involved others in making decisions about how the research will inform practice	☐	☐	☐	☐

(Continued)

Designing your research-informed change initiative	Not yet	Yes, but	Doing well	Not applicable now
Determined what adaptations might be needed to fit your context	☐	☐	☐	☐
Explored how others have contextualised and adapted research	☐	☐	☐	☐
Tested out your intended adaptations	☐	☐	☐	☐
Checked back to ensure that your intended approach aligns with the original research	☐	☐	☐	☐
Formed the rationale for your research-informed change initiative	☐	☐	☐	☐
Specified your intended outcomes	☐	☐	☐	☐
Determined how you will generate evidence of these outcomes	☐	☐	☐	☐
Developed the specific strategies, actions and resources that comprise your initiative	☐	☐	☐	☐
Clearly articulated your initiative in terms of: • What is involved; • Why you are taking this specific approach; and • Which changes you hope to see and how you are generating evidence of these changes	☐	☐	☐	☐

a. It may be that some of the checklist points are not applicable to your current focus, in which case, tick 'Not applicable now'. However, if they are relevant, we encourage you to record whether they are: not happening yet ('Not yet'), happening but with some challenges ('Yes, but'), or happening well ('Doing well').

ADDITIONAL REFLECTION
PRACTICE CHECKLIST CONSIDERATIONS

Use the space below to reflect on the following considerations. You can do this individually or with others.

- What results were surprising? Where is there room for growth?
- What changes could be made in response?
- Why are these changes important to you?

....

....

....

....

....

....

ADDITIONAL CASE STUDIES
ENGAGING THOUGHTFULLY WITH RESEARCH

To learn more about what thoughtful engagement with research looks like in action, you can engage with Steven and the #edureading group's case study about how they work with research as an online professional learning community (bit.ly/edureadingcasestudy) and/or Jessica's case study about the collective focus on inquiry in her primary school (bit.ly/jessicacasestudy).

You might like to respond to the considerations posed at the end of each case study and/or initiate a group discussion about one or both case studies in your school or organisation.

FURTHER READING
EXPLORING WAYS OF ENGAGING THOUGHTFULLY WITH RESEARCH

In Chapter 4, the Key Practices and Improvement Activity emphasised the importance of interpreting research to understand its practice implications and being considered in how you contextualise and translate research to your setting.

If you are interested in learning more about different ways of interpreting the implications of research and how it might be contextualised to your setting, you can read Timperley's (2012) *Building Professional Capability in School Improvement* conference paper (8 pages). It unpacks the type of inquiry cycle mentioned in Key Practice 1 and explains the questions asked at the different stages of the cycle.

ⓘ REFERENCES

Jones, K., & Wiliam, D. (2022). *Lethal mutations in education and how to prevent them*. Evidence-Based Education. https://evidencebased.education/lethal-mutations-in-education-and-how-to-prevent-them/

Timperley, H. (2012, August 27). *Building professional capability in school improvement* [Paper presentation]. School improvement: What does research tell us about effective strategies? Darling Harbour, New South Wales. https://research.acer.edu.au/research_conference/RC2012/27august/8

ⓘ SOURCES DISCUSSED BY EDUCATORS

If you would like more information on the sources mentioned by educators in Chapter 4, refer to the reference list below:

Berry, A. (2020). Disrupting to driving: Exploring upper primary teachers' perspectives on student engagement. *Teachers and Teaching: Theory and Practice*, *26*(2), 145–165. https://doi.org/10.1080/13540602.2020.1757421

De Bono, E. (2017). *Six thinking hats (Revised edition)*. Penguin. (Original work published in 1985)

Jensen, E. (2013). *Engaging students with poverty in mind: Practical strategies for raising achievement*. Association for Supervision and Curriculum Development (ASCD).

APPENDIX 5
IMPLEMENTING RESEARCH THOUGHTFULLY

ADDITIONAL ACTIVITY
PRACTICE CHECKLIST

Use the following checklist to determine how well you believe that you are currently applying the key practices outlined in Chapter 5.

You can complete this checklist yourself and use your responses to target 1–2 practices that you might want to improve. Or you might want to consider asking colleagues to read the chapter, complete the checklist and then initiate a group discussion to compare responses and potentially compile a collective improvement action plan.

Preparing for and planning implementation of research	Not yet	Yes, but	Doing well	Not applicable now[a]
Identified individuals and groups (and categorised by interest in/influence over implementation) to be engaged in implementation	☐	☐	☐	☐
Conducted an assessment of organisational readiness for implementation – taking into account the motivation of the people who will be implementing, and the general organisational and initiative-specific capacities required	☐	☐	☐	☐
Developed an implementation plan – taking into consideration the initiative itself, the implementation process and implementation outcomes	☐	☐	☐	☐

(Continued)

Implementing research-informed change thoughtfully	Not yet	Yes, but	Doing well	Not applicable now[a]
Determined need for and parameters of a trial	☐	☐	☐	☐
Executed the implementation plan for either a trial or the full implementation scope of the initiative	☐	☐	☐	☐
Engaged individuals and groups in the implementation process, delivery and evaluation	☐	☐	☐	☐
Gathered and evaluated feedback/data/evidence about implementation process effectiveness	☐	☐	☐	☐
Gathered and evaluated feedback/data/evidence about impact of trial/initiative	☐	☐	☐	☐
Gathered and evaluated feedback/data/evidence about people's engagement	☐	☐	☐	☐
Determined post-implementation next steps	☐	☐	☐	☐

a. It may be that some of the checklist points are not applicable to your current focus, in which case, tick 'Not applicable now'. However, if they are relevant, we encourage you to record whether they are: not happening yet ('Not yet'), happening but with some challenges ('Yes, but'), or happening well ('Doing well').

ADDITIONAL REFLECTION
PRACTICE CHECKLIST CONSIDERATIONS

Use the space below to reflect on the following considerations. You can do this individually or with others.

- What results were surprising? Where is there room for growth?
- What changes could be made in response?
- Why are these changes important to you?

ADDITIONAL CASE STUDY
PLANNING AND IMPLEMENTING A RESEARCH USE INITIATIVE

If you would like to read more about what thoughtful implementation of research looks like in action, you can engage with Tom's case study (bit.ly/tomcasestudy).

You might like to respond to the considerations posed at the end of the case study and/or initiate a group discussion about the case study in your school or organisation.

FURTHER READING
IMPLEMENTATION GUIDES

In Table 5.2 in Chapter 5, you were provided with an outline that you could use to plan the implementation (or trial) of a research-informed change initiative. As discussed in the chapter, several implementation guides have been recently published that you may want to consider reading. These are listed below and include publications by the Education Endowment Foundation (Sharples et al., 2019, 2024), and the Australian Education Research Organisation (AERO, 2024a,b).

REFERENCES

Australian Education Research Organisation (2024a). *Insights into implementation: What AERO is learning alongside schools about implementing evidence-based practices*. AERO. https://www.edresearch.edu.au/research/discussion-papers/insights-implementation

Australian Education Research Organisation (2024b). *Taking an evidence-informed approach to implementation*. AERO. https://www.edresearch.edu.au/summaries-explainers/explainers/taking-evidence-informed-approach-implementation

Scaccia, J. P., Cook, B. S., Lamont, A., Wandersman, A., Castellow, J., Katz, J., & Beidas, R. S. (2015). A practical implementation science heuristic for organizational readiness: R = MC^2. *Journal of Community Psychology*, *43*(4), 484–501. https://doi.org/10.1002/jcop.21698

Service, O., Hallsworth, M., Halpern, D., Algate, F., Gallagher, R., Nguyen, S., Ruda, S., Sanders, M., Pelenur, M., Gyani, A., Harper, H., Reinhard, J., & Kirkman, E. (2014). *EAST: Four simple ways to apply behavioural insights*. The Behavioural Insights Team. https://www.bi.team/publications/east-four-simple-ways-to-apply-behavioural-insights/

Sharples, J., Albers, B., & Fraser, S. (2019). *Putting evidence to work: A school's guide to implementation*. Education Endowment Foundation. https://d2tic4wvo1iusb.cloudfront.net/eef-guidance-reports/implementation/EEF_Implementation_Guidance_Report_2019.pdf

Sharples, J., Eaton, J., & Boughelaf, J. (2024). *A school's guide to implementation*. Education Endowment Foundation. https://educationendowmentfoundation.org.uk/education-evidence/guidance-reports/implementation

📎 APPENDIX 6
MODELLING QUALITY RESEARCH USE

ADDITIONAL ACTIVITY
PRACTICE CHECKLIST

Use the following checklist to determine how well you believe that you are currently applying the key practices outlined in Chapter 6.

You can complete this checklist yourself and use your responses to target 1–2 practices that you might want to improve. Or you might want to consider asking colleagues to read the chapter, complete the checklist and then initiate a group discussion to compare responses and potentially compile a collective improvement action plan.

You might also like to use the QURE Assessment Tool (bit.ly/quretool) to assess your own research use mindset, skillsets and relationships. This individual online assessment will take you approximately 10–15 minutes to complete, after which you will be immediately provided with a scoring profile that indicates your research use strengths as well as opportunities for you to build your capacities. Tailored scaffolds will be accessible, allowing you to plan for and action your improvement.

Investing time and effort in your own research use capacities	Not yet	Yes, but	Doing well	Not applicable now[a]
Made time in your schedule to engage with research	☐	☐	☐	☐
Consulted multiple research sources and types	☐	☐	☐	☐
Taken an "inquiry stance" to your own research use and leadership practices	☐	☐	☐	☐
Undertaken different forms of research use professional learning	☐	☐	☐	☐
Created a goal and/or action plan to improve your own research use capacities	☐	☐	☐	☐
Identified and consulted with colleagues who are currently studying to gain their insights into research	☐	☐	☐	☐
Connected with colleagues within or external to your school or organisation who are engaged with research to improve your knowledge/skills	☐	☐	☐	☐

(Continued)

Demonstrating quality research use to others	Not yet	Yes, but	Doing well	Not applicable now
Made your own research use practices and attitudes visible to others (e.g., in meetings)	☐	☐	☐	☐
Provided colleagues with exemplar research-informed materials (e.g., example lesson plans)	☐	☐	☐	☐
Demonstrated how to use research well (e.g., in professional learning or classroom settings)	☐	☐	☐	☐
Observed others trialling/ implementing research-informed practices and provided feedback	☐	☐	☐	☐
Curated and/or shared research or research-informed ideas with others	☐	☐	☐	☐
Created and/or leveraged organisational processes for knowledge sharing	☐	☐	☐	☐
Promoted the professional value of research use to others	☐	☐	☐	☐
Canvassed colleagues about research use and professionalism	☐	☐	☐	☐

a. It may be that some of the checklist points are not applicable to your current focus, in which case, tick 'Not applicable now'. However, if they are relevant, we encourage you to record whether they are: not happening yet ('Not yet'), happening but with some challenges ('Yes, but'), or happening well ('Doing well').

ADDITIONAL REFLECTION
PRACTICE CHECKLIST CONSIDERATIONS

Use the space below to reflect on the following considerations. You can do this individually or with others.

- What results were surprising? Where is there room for growth?
- What changes could be made in response?
- Why are these changes important to you?

....
....
....
....
....

ADDITIONAL CASE STUDIES
MODELLING QUALITY RESEARCH USE

If you would like to read more about what modelling quality research use looks like in action, you can engage with Marcus' (secondary school) (bit.ly/marcuscasestudy) and/or Bianca's (primary school) (bit.ly/biancacasestudy) case studies.

You might like to consider the questions posed at the end of each case study and/or initiate a group discussion about one or both case studies in your school or organisation.

FURTHER ACTIVITIES
BUILDING A RESEARCH-SHARING CULTURE

In Part 2 of the Improvement Activity in Chapter 6, you reflected on your own professional networks to identify colleagues or experts, both within and external to your school or organisation, who you could connect with to improve your research use knowledge and skills.

If you are interested in learning more about research sharing and receiving practices and how you can lead a knowledge sharing culture in your school or organisation, you might like to engage with the following resources:

- *Q Behavioural Insight* is a resource that shares a behavioural science perspective on using research well in practice. This Q Behavioural Insight discusses the different influences over sharing research behaviours and how you can bring about behavioural change in your school or organisation (bit.ly/qbehavioursharing).
- *Q Conversation* is a resource designed to promote discussion and reflection about research use attitudes and practices. This Q Conversation focuses on ways in which educators share and receive research (bit.ly/qconversationsharing) and includes an activity that encourages you to consider the ways in which your school or organisation shares and receives research and how you can improve your network connections.

FURTHER READING
QUALITY USE OF RESEARCH EVIDENCE (QURE) BEHAVIOURS

In Part 1 of the Improvement Activity in Chapter 6, you were asked to define some behaviour changes that you could make to improve your own research use capacities. This activity builds on the behaviour change work that you may have done in Chapter 2.

If you are interested in learning more about key behaviours that underpin the quality use of research and how these behaviours can be facilitated at individual (educator), organisational, and education system levels, you can read BehaviourWorks' report (Plant et al., 2022) (48 pages).

REFERENCE

Plant, B., Boulet, M., & Smith, L. (2022). *A behavioural approach to understanding and encouraging quality use of research evidence in Australian schools*. BehaviourWorks Australia. https://doi.org/10.26180/21530658

APPENDIX 7
SUPPORTING QUALITY RESEARCH USE

ADDITIONAL ACTIVITY
PRACTICE CHECKLIST

Use the following checklist to determine how well you believe that you are currently applying the key practices outlined in Chapter 7.

You can complete this checklist yourself and use your responses to target 1–2 practices that you might want to improve. Or you might want to consider asking colleagues to read the chapter, complete the checklist and then initiate a group discussion to compare responses and potentially compile a collective improvement action plan.

You might also like to engage with the QURE Assessment Tool (bit.ly/quretool) with colleagues to complete a group assessment of your team's or school's/organisation's research use. This group online assessment will take you approximately 5–10 minutes to set up and then 10–15 minutes for each participant to complete. Once the assessment is completed, you will be immediately provided with a scoring profile that indicates your group's research use strengths as well as opportunities for you (individually and/or collectively) to build your capacities. Tailored scaffolds will be accessible, allowing you to plan for and action improvement.

Providing tangible support for research use	Not yet	Yes, but	Doing well	Not applicable now[a]
Allocated time in teams' schedules to use research	☐	☐	☐	☐
Identified existing (or new) meetings to embed research use within	☐	☐	☐	☐
Built an online and/or physical research resource hub	☐	☐	☐	☐
Provided internal and access to external research use development opportunities	☐	☐	☐	☐
Created new or leveraged existing inquiry cycles and/or professional learning community structures for research use	☐	☐	☐	☐
Created dedicated positions for supporting others to improve their research use	☐	☐	☐	☐
Created new or leveraged other organisational structures/processes to focus on research use-related coaching/mentoring	☐	☐	☐	☐

Building a supportive culture for research use	Not yet	Yes, but	Doing well	Not applicable now
Encouraged individuals and groups to experiment with research	☐	☐	☐	☐
Created new or leveraged existing organisational structures/processes to allow for research-informed practice trials	☐	☐	☐	☐
Created new or leveraged existing instructional/distributed leadership models to help people improve their research use	☐	☐	☐	☐
Shared research use leadership responsibility with others	☐	☐	☐	☐
Shared and/or celebrated examples of research use successes	☐	☐	☐	☐

a. It may be that some of the checklist points are not applicable to your current focus, in which case, tick 'Not applicable now'. However, if they are relevant, we encourage you to record whether they are: not happening yet ('Not yet'), happening but with some challenges ('Yes, but') or happening well ('Doing well').

ADDITIONAL REFLECTION
PRACTICE CHECKLIST CONSIDERATIONS

Use the space below to reflect on the following considerations. You can do this individually or with others.

- What results were surprising? Where is there room for growth?
- What changes could be made in response?
- Why are these changes important to you?

....

....

....

....

....

ADDITIONAL CASE STUDY
SUPPORTING QUALITY RESEARCH USE

To find out more about supporting quality research use, you can engage with Seadale Primary School's case study (bit.ly/seadalecasestudy) about establishing research use infrastructure.

You might like to respond to the considerations posed at the end of the case study and/or initiate a group discussion about the case study in your school or organisation.

FURTHER ACTIVITY
STRENGTHENING YOUR ORGANISATIONAL RESEARCH USE CULTURE

In Chapter 7, Key Practice 2 outlined three ways that you can build a supportive research use culture in your school or organisation

To promote discussion about building and leading a quality research use culture, you might like to engage with our *Q Conversation* that focuses on strengthening organisational infrastructure (bit.ly/qconversationinfrastructure). It features an activity that encourages you to consider your own organisational culture and what actions you can take to strengthen the ways in which you support people's evidence and research use.

FURTHER INFORMATION
KEY CONCEPTS

In Chapter 7, you were introduced to the key practice of providing tangible supports to help others improve their research use. The following key concepts box explains the difference between types of support.

TYPES OF RESEARCH USE SUPPORT

- **Material support**: In our work, access to appropriate research and scheduled time within working hours to engage with it were two of the most significant ways that schools or organisations can materially support their staff to use research well. Other types of material support include: access to in-house research or resource centres, platforms or libraries; access to specifically curated research; access to supporting resources such as research use 'how-to' guides; funded subscriptions to academic databases/journals and/or professional publications; and funded memberships to professional associations.

- **Developmental support**: Dimmock (2016, 2019) explains that for a research-engaged school culture to build, leaders have an accountability to provide support in the form of developmental opportunities, experiences and structures so that staff can improve their research use skills and knowledge. In our work, these types of developmental supports included: professional learning opportunities, both formal and informal, and either experienced within and/or external to the school or organisation; access to in-house research use lead roles or coaches; access to external mentors and advisors; access to university-organisation partnerships; attendance and/or presentations made at conferences; participation in peer or leader-led demonstrations; and participation in research-based cycles of inquiry, professional learning communities or similar developmental meetings and structures.

FURTHER READING
QUALITY USE OF RESEARCH EVIDENCE (QURE) BEHAVIOURS AND BEHAVIOURAL CHANGE

In Parts 1 and 2 of the Improvement Activity in Chapter 7, you were asked to identify research use actions that you would like to support in your context, and then explore different ways in which you could support these. This activity builds on the behaviour change work that you may have done in Chapters 2 and 6.

If you are interested in learning more about key behaviours that underpin the quality use of research and how you can lead behavioural change in your school or organisation, you can read:

- BehaviourWorks' report about *A Behavioural Approach to Understanding and Encouraging Quality Use of Research Evidence* (Plant et al., 2022) (48 pages); and
- The Behavioural Insights Team's report about facilitating behavioural change using the *EAST Framework* (Service et al., 2014) (53 pages).

REFERENCES

Dimmock, C. (2016). Conceptualising the research-practice-professional development nexus: Mobilising schools as 'research-engaged' professional learning communities. *Professional Development in Education, 42*(1), 36–53. https://doi.org/10.1080/19415257.2014.963884

Dimmock, C. (2019). Leading research-informed practice in schools. In D. Godfrey & C. Brown (Eds.), *An ecosystem for research-engaged schools: Reforming education through research* (pp. 56–72). Routledge. https://doi.org/10.4324/9780203701027-5

Plant, B., Boulet, M., & Smith, L. (2022). *A behavioural approach to understanding and encouraging quality use of research evidence in Australian schools*. BehaviourWorks Australia. https://doi.org/10.26180/21530658.v1

Service, O., Hallsworth, M., Halpern, D., Algate, F., Gallagher, R., Nguyen, S., Ruda, S., Sanders, M., Pelenur, M., Gyani, A., Harper, H., Reinhard, J., & Kirkman, E. (2014). *EAST: Four simple ways to apply behavioural insights*. The Behavioural Insights Team. https://www.bi.team/publications/east-four-simple-ways-to-apply-behavioural-insights/

INDEX

Note: Page numbers in **bold** and *italics* refer to tables and figures, respectively.

academic databases 50–52, **51**, 195
adaptation of research **76**, 87–92
appropriate research 42–43, 58–66, 175–177; accessing research 57; case study 56–66; context, aspects of 45–46; contextual factors 45, **45**; evidence *4*, 4–6; formats 48, **49**; intend to use 43–45; results of 53; school-level factors **45**; selection 42; sources of research **51**; staff-level factors **45**; student-level factors **45**; trustworthy and relevant 43–49, **47**, 56–57; wide and strategic research 50–55; *see also* research, effective use of
Association for Supervision and Curriculum Development 57
ATACT (actor, target, action, context, time) framework *35*, 36–38, *37*, *132*, 132–134

behaviours *35*; identifying research use 35–37; purpose of research use 37–39
Berry, Amy 81, 90

classroom practices 2–3; messiness of 75
colleagues and experts, collaboration with 20
communication 25; style and content 25
comparative research 44, 178
consulting others, benefits **21**
context, aspects of 45–46
culture *4*, 4–5

data-based evidence 174
de Bono's thinking hats 73
descriptive research 44, 178
developmental opportunities 121
discerning decisions 73

EAST (easy, attractive, social and timely) framework 156–159
educational improvement for students 5–6
educational practices 3
education systems 6
Engaging Students with Poverty in Mind (Jensen) 57
evidences: data-based evidence 174; hubs **51**; interrogated from different angles 20; over time 20; practice-based evidence 174; process of analysing 21; research-based evidence 174; sources 19
experimental research 43, 60, 178
expertise, development of 165–166
external sources of support for research use **122**

filters 53

guiding questions for yourself 19

implementation: engaging others 104–106; readiness, aspects of **98**; trials 102–104, **103–104**
infrastructure 4, *4*

Jensen, Eric 57

keywords for your searches 52–53
knowledge: pull 6; push 6; sharing culture 125–126

leadership *4*, 4–5; action 118; mindset 151; practice of modelling quality research 118

learning, importance of 164
lethal mutations 77

meetings 142; embedding research use 142
mindsets *4*, 4–5
modelling quality research use *see* quality research, modelling
Monash Q Project 3, 10

NAPLAN [national numeracy and literacy assessment] data 20
need for improvement 19–20, 24, 27–28
Nutley, S. M. 179

one-on-one coaching 151
operators, search strings and **53**
organisational cultures 118

practice-based evidence 174
practice hub 151
professionalism 163; of educators 6
professional learning 120–121
professional networks 51–52
Professional relationships with others 122
professional value of research use 126–127
promotion, consistent and strategic 26; framework 26; processes 26; purpose for research 26
purpose of research 18–19, 171–174; aspects 18; case study 27–29; identification 24–25, 27, 30–35; identifying behaviours 24–25, 30–37; need for improvement 19–20, 27–28, 31–33; perspectives 20–21; promoting and explaining **24**, 24–25, 28–29; specific need **22**, 22–23

Q Conversation 153
Q Data Insight 179
quality research: actions to support 154–157; behaviours to support 157–159; in education systems 6; use capacities and practices 118–119

quality research, modelling 118–119, 124–127, 131, 185–191; in action 128–129; case study 128–131; connections 134–135; investing time and effort 132–134; opportunities within organization 136–137; quality research, demonstrating 124–127; research use skills and practices 120–121; strengthening capacity 119–123
Quality Use of Research Evidence (QURE) Assessment Tool 3, *4*, 121, 144, 153, 174, 191–192, 196

relationships *4*, 4–5
research, effective use of 2–3, 18, **44**, 169; characteristics 6–7, *8*; complications in 6–7; defined 3; developmental practice 7, *8*; expertise 165–167; hidden practice 7, *8*; importance 5–6; integrated practice 6–7, *8*; journey 162–163; learning 163–164; overview 3–5; poorly supported practice 7, *8*; sophisticated practice 6, *8*; *see also* appropriate research
research, engaging thoughtfully 68–69; adaptations 75; being reflective and discerning 72–74; case study 81–84; colleagues, making decisions with 73; contextualising and translating 75–80; critical thinking 69–72; existing professional learning processes 72; implications 69–74; insights fit with other research 71; interpretation 69–74; practice checklist 181–183; questions of the research publications 70, **70**; taking your time 71; thinking about research itself 68; working collaboratively 71–72; work with the research 68
research, implementing thoughtfully 96–97; actions, motivations and capacity 110–113; case study 107–109; delivering and sustaining 96; engaging others 113–115; implementation plan outline **101**; implementation trials 102–104;

informed change 102–106, 109–113; practice checklist 185–187; preparing for 97–101
research, scanning and selecting 53–54
research-based evidence 174
research-based learning opportunities 127
research-engaged culture 140
research-engaged mindset 119–120
research evidence 3; generation and translation 6
research-informed changes 19, 69, 99; initiative 68, **79**, 96
research-informed curriculum 148
research-informed improvement 6
research-informed initiative 98; trialling **103–104**
research-informed teaching practice **76**, 124, 146
research-related resources **143**
research repositories **51**
resource hubs 143, **143**
role-modelling quality research use 124

school curriculum 25
search strings and operators **53**
skillsets *4*, 4–5
SMART [specific, measurable, achievable, realistic and time-bound] goals 144
supporting, leading by 140–141; in action 150–152; case study 150–152; celebrating successes 148–149; developmental support 195; distributed leadership for research use 147–148; encouraging others 147; experimentation 146–147; identification 154–159; involving others in leading quality research use 147–148; material support 195; meetings, embedding research use in 141–142; organisational culture 146–149; organisational structures and processes 144–145; organisational support 140; organisation-wide commitment 148; in practice 153; practice checklist 153, 193–195; research resource hub 143; tangible support 141–145
systematic reviews 43, 174, 178
system-level influences *4*, 4–5

tangible supports for research use 140
teacher-student interactions 2–3
thoughtful engagement and implementation 4, *4*
thoughtfulness of research 5
time and effort in strengthening research 123
trust 148
trying out 102

Universal Design for Learning (UDL) framework 19–20

For Product Safety Concerns and Information please contact our EU
representative GPSR@taylorandfrancis.com
Taylor & Francis Verlag GmbH, Kaufingerstraße 24, 80331 München, Germany

www.ingramcontent.com/pod-product-compliance
Lightning Source LLC
Chambersburg PA
CBHW071819230426
43670CB00013B/2502